ACT

ACT

The Modern Actor's Handbook

DAVID ROTENBERG

Published by ECW Press

665 Gerrard Street East
Toronto, Ontario, Canada M4M 1Y2
416-694-3348 / info@ecwpress.com

Editors for the Press: Alison Clarke, Jen Knoch
Cover design: David Drummond
Author photo: John Reeves
Interior illustrations: Christopher Rouleau

LIBRARY AND ARCHIVES CANADA
CATALOGUING IN PUBLICATION

Title: Act : the modern actor's handbook
/ David Rotenberg.

Names: Rotenberg, David (David
Charles), author.

Identifiers: Canadiana (print)
20200385011 | Canadiana (ebook)
20200385151

ISBN 978-1-77041-468-6 (SOFTCOVER)
ISBN 978-1-77305-729-3 (EPUB)
ISBN 978-1-77305-730-9 (PDF)
ISBN 978-1-77305-731-6 (KINDLE)

Subjects: LCSH: Acting. | LCSH:
Acting—Vocational guidance. | LCSH:
Acting—Auditions.

Classification: LCC PN2055 .R68 2021 |
DDC 792.02/8—dc23

This book is funded in part by the Government of Canada. *Ce livre est financé en partie par le
gouvernement du Canada.* We acknowledge the contribution of the Government of Ontario
through the Ontario Book Publishing Tax Credit, and through Ontario Creates for the
marketing of this book.

PRINTED AND BOUND IN CANADA

PRINTING: MARQUIS   5   4   3   2   1

TABLE OF CONTENTS

ACKNOWLEDGMENTS

I could not have even begun writing a book like this if it wasn't for the hundreds of talented actors who allowed me into their hearts and minds. It was, and remains, a real honor to be in the room with many of these talented artists. In the long run, I probably learned more from them than they ever learned from me.

Much of what follows are distillations of what they taught me.

Many have graciously allowed me to participate in their terrific successes. Many others still valiantly "beat on, boats against the current," kept afloat by the love of the art of acting.

This book is a way of thanking those actors.

Then there are the fine teachers who work at my studio, The Professional Actors Lab — Bruce, Marvin, Rae Ellen, Jeff, Laurel, Andrea, Phyllis and Noam.

As always, this book is for Susan, Joey and Beth — but now I am happy to add Mary and Bean.

A NOTE ON THE USE OF
PRONOUNS IN THIS TEXT

I have tried to keep things gender neutral in the book. But at times I slip and use gendered pronouns. In those instances, I am not inferring that one gender is preferable.

A WORD OR TWO OF INTRODUCTION

"Stories can reveal the truth even if they are not truthful."

— GRAFFITI ON THE CANAL STREET
SUBWAY WALL, CIRCA 1976

I have taught professional actors for over thirty years. I began teaching between directing gigs in regional theaters when I was trying to stop smoking, hence no more work in bars. Yes, they allowed smoking in bars back then. I taught in my Manhattan apartment three nights a week — my wife was very patient. In my second year of teaching I was contacted by a young man from Yonkers. He asked if I would set up a class for him and three of his friends. I asked about his background. He was not strictly an amateur, but he was clearly not traveling on a traditional professional trajectory. What he clearly was, was hungry. So I agreed.

On that first night he showed up with his three friends, one of whom was a dark-eyed young woman whose anger was so close to the surface that her face was in almost constant motion. That initial class we talked through some basic concepts, did a bit of improvisation and broke down a simple scene. Because the young woman decided that she wanted to "just watch" I suggested the three men prepare something from David Mamet's *American Buffalo* for next week.

As they left, they put the money for class on the coffee table. It was obvious to me that the money they gave me was their food money. It was a moment that I have never forgotten.

I watched them from my brownstone window as they trudged through the snow and grime toward the Lexington Avenue subway.

When I picked up the money they'd left for me I immediately thought of the responsibility it imposed on me, and, to be frank, it frightened me.

It was the beginning of my thinking that it was no longer good enough to deliver hashed-over versions of the old acting tropes. Their food money obliged me to relook at what it was that I was teaching and had been taught, and upon closer examination and research I was shocked at how little serious reassessing had been done in the field. How few changes had been made to the classic acting texts, despite the clear fact that an actor's world had changed drastically. More on that later.

The following week my Yonkers actors announced that they were ready to show me *American Buffalo*. I said sure, assuming that they had put a few pages of the play on its feet. They started into the play — from the top. They did the whole play, cover to cover, without a break. What they did manage to break in the course of their performance was the mirror over the mantlepiece, a lamp and a windowpane. When they were finished, they turned to me as if to ask, "So, what do you think, Coach?"

What I thought was that hunger was an essential part of being a professional actor and that these young actors deserved more than the old acting dogma I'd been taught.

One of these four aggressive young actors eventually barged his way into the profession. The other two men gave up the fight after a few years. The young woman — well, it's been my experience that anger can be a terribly destructive emotion when it is not understood.

That was one of the few times in my life that I taught beginners. I still don't teach beginners, and this book is not intended for beginning actors, although if they have enough hunger, they'll be able to find their own way of using the ideas and methods in these pages.

Like most good ideas, the concepts in this book are easy to learn but may take a lifetime to master. Because nothing of any value can be put on a 3 by 5 index card — except the thought that "Nothing of any value can be put on a 3 by 5 index card."

Acting teaching can be roughly broken down into those explorations that are about finding notes on an actor's emotional piano keyboard and those explorations that are about how to play those notes. This book, and my work for the past thirty plus years, is primarily about the latter: how to play the notes you have found; how to understand what your notes mean; which of your notes are no longer any good; which have been false from the beginning; which notes can replace bad notes; which notes are available to you but you don't know about either because they are in a blind spot or are yet to be discovered; and, most importantly, how to play the notes you have in a fashion that, as Shakespeare says, "will discourse most eloquent music" (*Hamlet*, act 3, sc. 2).

I have often envied piano teachers — at least their students can see the notes they need to play. As an acting teacher you must suss out the notes in an actor and then, as Hamlet says to Rosencrantz and Guildenstern, "know my stops ... pluck out the heart of my mystery ... sound me from my lowest note to the top of my compass" (act 3, sc. 2). In fact, that is exactly what an actor does — the actor knows their stops and plays them in such a way that they produce "most eloquent music" that shares "the heart of [their] mystery" with the viewing public.

The actor's territory is the human heart. It is an uncharted land sometimes defended by terrifying dragons, but it also contains great glories, music and deep human truths. To the hungry actor it is the only land worthy of investigation.

This book, *ACT*, attempts to give the actor a compass and a few points of entry into that divine territory. It is a journey that, for an artist, lasts a lifetime.

A QUICK WORD ABOUT TECHNIQUE

This book is full of techniques. I don't expect every actor to use every one of them for preparation or performance. Technique, all technique, is there for an artist when the way forward seems terribly confused; when you can't get past the exploration stage; when the voice in your head reading you your lines is all you can come up with; when, although others are pleased with your work, as the star of the series you are bored, bored, bored with it; when you find yourself coming up with the same product over and over again; when others always seem to be getting the role you want; when you finally at long last commit yourself to making your work compelling.

However, if you are *not* lost, and instead are functioning on all cylinders, feeling tall, feeling beautiful, feeling loved (you pick the one that gets you going), then no technique of any sort should be used. Just breathe down, pull out those back ribs and remember it is an honor to be paid to do the thing you love.

But remember: use technique when you are lost *not* when you are found.

There are certain categories of actors who shouldn't use technique at all. This is actually the rule of thumb for very young and very old actors. They are compelling by the nature of their respective ages. They can get away with doing straight drops and don't have to be sophisticated about the playing of their notes, they just need to play them honestly and by so doing reveal to the audience the glories and secrets of either youth or age.

A few times in a professional actor's life they will play a role where everything makes sense — "fuck, man, this is my life, my dreams!" When this happens (and it doesn't happen very often) you will find that every time the director explains something to you, you understand it less and all you want to do is "shoot this fucker!" (Name that film, oh great film buffs.) These are moments of peak performance and should be enjoyed fully for what they are: gifts from the gods who are much better known for their cruelty than their generosity.

These should not be mistaken for moments of inspiration. Inspiration is for amateurs. A professional actor performs compellingly even when the script is crap, your acting partner is phoning it in long distance person-to-person collect (I grant this is an archaic reference), the director is an idiot and the design was clearly the realization of a person recently released from Charenton. (Google it.)

A professional actor accesses the art of acting even in the foulest of circumstances. It is the job. It is what the techniques in this book are for.

On a serious note: I never try to get actors to give

up techniques that work for them, but take a look at the ideas in this book and see if you want to add them to your kitbag. You never know when they might come in handy.

A QUICK WORD ABOUT THE BIZ

A professional actor knows that the business of acting must not be ignored. However, if your acting degenerates into a series of business concerns, then you have lost something of inestimable value.

If there is no art to acting, there is no reason to do it.

There are much better businesses than acting, and much simpler crafts. A modestly talented waiter might make more money, in the long run, than a modestly talented actor — and they will not experience the intensity of rejection that is the common lot of the professional actor. But an actor is involved in an art form — something that can take a life to master.

When I lived in New York I frequented a few bars because their bartenders were actually actors or dancers or musicians who were only tending bar while waiting for their careers to begin. I'll never forget one cold afternoon when I went back to one specific bar whose bartender was a violinist. I entered and was shocked to see my bartender — something had died. She was no longer a violinist tending bar; she was now a bartender. A dream had vaporized and her eyes had lost their luster.

An artist tending bar is not the same as a bartender. One is devoted to an art, one is not.

An actor must understand the business of acting but must not fall prey to the idea that the business is the art — or that finding tricks to get ahead in the business is the job of the professional actor. It isn't.

CHAPTER 1

Getting Present

GLENNA: You're in a peppy mood today.

EDMOND: You're goddamn right I am, and you want me to tell you *why*? Because I am *alive*. You know how much of our life we're alive, you and me? *Nothing*. Two minutes out of the year . . . we live in a fog. We live in a dream. Our life is a *school*house, and we're dead . . . I've lived in a fog thirty-four years. Most of the life I have to live. It's gone. It's gone. I wasted it. Because I didn't know. And you know what the answer is? To *live*.
— *EDMOND* BY DAVID MAMET, SCENE 15

"If I don't fall in love three times from the moment I leave my trailer to the time I get to camera setup, I'm not ready to work," said one of my more famous private acting clients — whose name I will not share with you.

And no, he was not talking about pawing or approaching people. He was talking about allowing himself to get Present enough to see the beauty of the faces all around him. It was his way of checking to be sure that he was really Present.

THE NEED TO BE PRESENT

Let's start with something tough: *IF YOU CAN'T GET PRESENT YOU CAN'T ACT!* Period, the end. Pas de plus. Of all the contentious things I say in classes, and I say many things that are contentious, I never back off from that statement even an inch. No technique of any sort, the ones in this book included, will help your acting if you can't get Present.

The most important gift that an actor brings to the feast is the ability to get Present on command. Almost all of you had this gift when you were children. When a baby looks at you, they really look at you. When a child is hurt, they really feel the pain. When a kid is told they are stupid, it slays them. All because they are Present. They're really there. They really hear. They really see. And it all goes in through their eyes and ears, plunges to their hearts and either thrills or kills them. They are Present.

In the '60s classic cult novel *Stranger in a Strange Land,* several women sit in a room discussing why this one guy is special. One of the women finally comes up with, "When you kiss this guy, he really kisses you back. He's all there." Right — he's Present.

An actor needs to be Present because they must see and hear like the narrator in a great Russian novel. That's why we follow them. They encounter the same joys and pains that you and I encounter, but we pass through them, they stop and experience them.

Being Present sits in stark opposition to the survival skills that life teaches in order to keep us safe. Being Present requires that you live your life so as to feel your life, not live your life so as to avoid pain. In *Zorba the Greek*, Kazantzakis makes the distinction between the young Englishman who lives his life "as if he might die tomorrow" as opposed to Zorba who lives his life "knowing full well that he could die tomorrow." Zorba lives in Present tense, his young English companion does not.

It is dangerous to be Present for the simple reason that when you are Present others have real access to you, your feelings and your secrets — and they can hurt you if they choose.

For that reason, being Present requires bravery, centeredness (which is not the same as arrogance, but is the confidence borne of knowing one's own worth) and a leap of faith.

Talented directors (and there are not all that many around) don't need to see an actor read lines to know if they are in the presence of an actor. They can tell that the person entering the room is an actor because, unlike the rest of the people in the room, themself often included, the actor is *Present*. Present enough to impose on us that the story of the play, film or teleplay runs through them, the river is theirs. The tributaries may be interesting but only feed the river — the actor.

Geoffrey Hyland, an extraordinarily gifted acting teacher at the University of Cape Town, said while I was teaching for him that "a great actor not only hears the words his acting partner says but also the intent behind those words and one free association deeper than the intent. A great actor when looking straight into his acting partner's eyes sees not only the face in front of him but also the sides and the back of his acting partner's head." And this cannot be done unless you are Present.

As Mr. Mamet implies in the section of his play *Edmond* that is quoted at the top of this chapter, we are not Present for much of our lives. If we, the audience, were Present, we would not need much of what the actor has to offer. We watch actors act to better understand the happenings of our everyday lives and the events of lives that are outside the realms of our experience.

Part of the job of the artist is to expose the extraordinary in the ordinary and the ordinary in the extraordinary. And these exposures can only take place if the actor is Present.

It is the actor's ability to remain fully Present in moments that the rest of us could not, that allows them to open up a life event for our edification.

NOT BEING PRESENT IN EVERYDAY LIFE

It is not an accident that during the great breakup scenes of our lives — many of which take place in bedrooms, some of which occur while we are wearing far too little clothing — that we, the person being broken up with, are unable to find our words. It is only later, when walking down the darkened hallway, pulling on a shirt, that it occurs to us that we should have said this when they said that, and when they called us that we should have called them this. Also, during the long walk to the car, we find that we can't exactly recall the sequence of events or the turn of phrase — all because we were not totally Present during the event. And thank goodness! Even in our half-comatose state — "in a fog," as Mr. Mamet puts it — some of the nastier cracks still penetrate to the point that they may stay with us for a lifetime.

We enter the fog because our personal survival tools have moved forward to protect us, as well they should — if you are a civilian. As an actor, the job is to stay Present during the entirety of the breakup, to experience all the "slings and arrows," if you will, and allow us to see and hear what it feels like from the safe distance of the theater's darkness or our living room couch.

When the TV reporter sticks his microphone under the face of the poor woman who has just lost a child in a fire and asks, "How do you feel?" she doesn't know what to say because, gratefully, the woman feels nothing. She's not Present, thank goodness. The pain will, over time, seep through the holes in the armor of her survival system. Her profound sense of loss will be spurred by a shadow in a store window, a flake of snow that lands on her nose or an empty chair in the corner of a thrift shop. Or perhaps by nothing at all, just time itself eating away at her protection.

An actor playing the very same scene is not allowed to fall into the realism that is "the fog" but must stay Present. It is part of what we pay an actor to do. Take a look at Edward Norton's performance in *American History X* when the reporter asks him how he feels after his father, a fireman, was murdered. There is no distance or time between the announcement of loss and the outpouring of grief. Mr. Norton remains throughout the scene, correctly so, in Present tense, and hence the response is instantaneous, painful and very hard to watch.

The words "repercussion" and "ramification" play almost no role when you are Present.

I have often told actors in my studio that if they had been Present on their way to class that they would never have gotten there. While Present, if another car cuts you off, you hit the accelerator, not the brake. If you are Present and pass by a poor soul on the street asking for a bit of spare change, you give them your wallet, your shoes, your firstborn . . . and you don't make it to class. We don't live our real lives in Present tense, nor should we.

In some cities it is easier to find Present tense. When I lived in Manhattan in the late '70s and '80s it was relatively easy to get Present. The city was seething with both energy and anger, and if you didn't keep your wits about you, you could easily end up in trouble. But even in New York City people adapted and returned to a form of sleepwalking to get through their days, at times simply to avoid the pain that was all around them.

But an artist isn't allowed to sleep through their lives. Even when they aren't working, they are required to drop into being Present, to experience their day. Tuesday must not feel like Saturday, February and August are not the same. Eccentricity and horror are not alike.

Civilians avoid being Present because the major dictum of modern life is: avoid pain. If you are Present you will feel the pain. If you are Present, by the by, you may also feel the joy.

Most people find a moment of being Present when they are in a movie theater with someone new as the lights begin to go down. All of a sudden everything matters: it matters that she crossed her legs left to right; it matters that he bought popcorn with the gooey crap on it; it matters that the two teens in front of you are talking dirty; it matters that the short is *Trout Fishing in Quebec*. (Name that film reference!) If everything matters, you're Present.

Here's an example of how Present tense is different from the way we live our lives. Your front doorbell rings. You answer it and there are twelve fresh-cut, long-stemmed roses. You unwrap them and put them in water, and add an aspirin if you believe in that. Instantly their fragrance fills the room and your system comes instantly alive and registers: roses! Within thirty seconds, although your nose still smells the roses, your mind refuses to register them. Your mind has filed the smell away as roses, but unimportant, so it doesn't bother you with the fact of the smell. When you are Present you smell the roses *all the time*.

When you put an olive into a baby's mouth — as I did with our son Joey while he was still in a high chair — the child gets Present as he tries to figure out what in heaven's name this taste is! He needs to open up a new file in his head, the olive file. Doing so also makes him Present.

Artists need to force their senses into being awake (smelling the roses, tasting the olive) on a regular basis just to keep the artistic impulse alive. It requires no more than a walk or a serious look at your kitchen, as long as you will yourself to believe that what you see and hear *really matters*. You really look and listen, really see and hear.

Civilians often make major life decisions while basically asleep (Mamet's "in a fog") and therefore don't really know how they got from holding hands to two kids, two cars and a mortgage. They go to the theater or turn on their televisions to watch actors, in Present tense, enact the hundreds of scenes between the touch of hands and the twentieth wedding anniversary. Great actors help us understand what is happening and has happened in our lives.

WHAT EXACTLY IS BEING PRESENT?

Being Present is the state wherein all the data inputs around you register and touch your heart.

It is not the same as athletes talking about being "in the zone," which has to do with the accessing body memory to the exclusion of the external world. Being Present surely does fully access body memory, but it also registers the world — and, in certain circumstances, one's place in that world.

It is also not that thing that Stephen King describes in *Misery* when he talks about falling into the computer screen when writing, where time seems to not matter, nor does food — or much of anything else. I have eleven novels in bookstores and know exactly, what that feeling is — but that is not being Present in the acting sense of that term.

If you are a poker player, and God has been good to you, on rare evenings you have found yourself at the card table knowing that when Harold doubles his bet, he is bluffing; that Robert is going to try to draw to an inside straight even though he sees that one of the sevens he needs is showing in another player's up cards; that the contour of the fabric on the table is more worn in front of the player to your right than in front of the player to your left; that the light overhead is off center to the table; that you really wish Larry would wash his hands before he dealt the cards; that clearly Carl and his wife are not getting along; and that Claire always needs to blow her nose when she gets a good hand, although clearly what she would like to do is move the two jacks on the left side of her hand to the one jack on the right side. Time seems to slow just a bit and sounds register more clearly and everything cross-references with both feeling *and* understanding.

The extraordinary thing that poker players know as that "feeling" can go away as quickly and as mysteriously as it arrived. When you see players in this state, they don't want to take bathroom breaks, they want the betting limit raised and they really don't want to break for pastrami on rye no matter how much they love deli.

These are moments of peak performance and are closely analogous to being Present.

From the outside the manifestation of an actor being Present should be obvious. The basic reediness of everyday speech is produced from the air in the very top of the lungs. But when an actor gets Present, their voice will fall into place. Their breath will drop to their back ribs, which magically they will find they can move out on command. Their voice will come from there without being deep which is how voices should be. As well, his quintessential self will move forward into his facial bones thus making him significantly more attractive than usual.

The religious manifestation of being Present has to do with sensing the turning of the earth and a deep understanding of one's place in an ever-spinning cosmos.

Being Present is an unnatural state for most people.

Those who are infinitely comfortable being Present seldom make good actors because being constantly Present has a tendency to destroy your personal life and this business is too hard for those who can't manage to have some stability in their life away from the set.

The ability to access Present tense on demand is something that actors work on from the beginning of their training until they make their final appearances, because once an actor finds Present tense it can quickly become something else — not Present but false Present. So, the exploration begins again — like a person lost in a vast white room, searching to find the door out. When they finally find it, they step out only to find themselves in even a vaster, whiter room. These are the explorations of artists.

GETTING ACTORS PRESENT

Getting actors Present is a major job, but it is the job of those who teach beginning actors. It is literally the introduction of the actor to his or her emotional piano keyboard. It takes time, patience, persistence and some-times a willingness to cross over into a student's privacy. Some acting systems concentrate almost entirely on get-ting students Present. Some of the famous acting studios in New York City and Los Angeles do little else. It is crucial work. But it is beginners' work. However, once again, if you can't get Present you can't act — period.

A professional actor knows that getting Present is a totally unnatural thing. There is nothing natural about naturalistic acting. That's why acting is an art. According to the Online Etymology Dictionary "art" means "skill as a result of learning or practice" *and* "skill in cunning and trickery." (Hence the terms "artificial" and "artifice" coming from the same Greek root that gave us the word "art.")

It is in fact the need for Present tense that can make teaching acting such an uncomfortable fit in some univer-sities. When an acting student finally finds Present tense you really can't demand that they watch their mouths, are careful with their physicality, avoid impulses or are even vaguely politically correct. It's why acting studios are private places. The actor needs a safe place to contact the "unsafe" parts of themselves — to understand those places and keep them in a box and under control when in the civilian world. When they are Present they are fully accessing the entirety of their hidden life experience. And deep in almost everyone's hidden life experience reside some pretty complicated things.

When an actor opens the door to being Present, beasts of all sorts may enter the world. And many of those beasts are crucial notes on the actor's piano keyboard and therefore are needed by professional actors.

I directed the first Canadian play in the People's Republic of China in 1994 (in Mandarin I might add). Shanghai at the time was just awakening from fifty years of neglect from Beijing and had seventy-eight of the largest holes in the ground that shortly became seventy-eight of the newest tall buildings in the world. They had one subway station but no subway trains. There was little English spoken and all street signs were in characters, so I was lost a great deal of the time. There were very few cars — tons of bikes, but very few cars. However, the third time that a driver almost ran me down, I stood in the midst of Nanjing Lu (one of the busiest streets in the world) and out came words about Chinese people that I didn't ever realize that I knew. Thankfully no one in hearing distance must have spoken English — I was obviously just some crazy long nose (white person) who didn't know how to cross the damned street! It was an awful moment of the darkness coming out into the light. Actors need access to the darkness for their art, *not* for their lives.

A NOTE OR TWO ON TEACHING GETTING PRESENT

The next problem actors face is that they need to get Present independent of the playing of actions, speaking lines or moving about. Again, actors need to get Present without text or scene partners. They have to be able to find a comfort zone within the unsettling, shifting, falling demands of being Present. They need to get used to the notion that every face is intrinsically beautiful — and grotesquely ugly. That we live our lives utterly alone despite our desperate efforts to find connection. That things can and should affect them deeply.

The initial moments of being Present are often deeply disturbing for a young actor. They lose the sense of the word "repercussion" and find themselves adrift in a world of their own needs and whims. They also find themselves both attracted to and repelled by many of the people in the studio. It's complicated because all of an actor's life experience has told them to stay away from exposing themselves like this.

But without being Present there is no great acting. Sorry. There is no acting.

In an effort to get the actor Present, the teacher must be careful not to be judgmental. An acting class is a lousy place to deal with complex personal problems, and is arguably the very worst place to correct any form of mental imbalance. Acting teachers are not psychologists, social workers or shrinks. Their concern is the art of acting, not the maintenance of, or return to, mental health. The acting teacher's concern is whether the actor can get Present enough to harness the boldness of their hidden selves to the work. Whether that boldness is correct or healthy is beyond an acting teacher's purview. If the actor's personal problems incapacitate them, then those problems must be dealt with outside of the studio by a professional. But if the problems do not incapacitate the actor, then the problems just become something else that needs to be included in the work.

PROBLEM TERRITORY

Acting teachers only need to venture into this "problem" territory when blocks in the actor are stopping them from accessing important knowledge. To use the piano key metaphor yet again, if the note that frightens (incapacitates) the actor is the F# two octaves below middle C, then the actor must know that the F natural and the E and the G two octaves down from middle C are not problems. So the actor can't play the F# two octaves down from middle C. Fine. I've never met an actor who has all the notes on the piano. What an actor needs to know is which notes are dragons. Which notes are so frightening that they will shut down their system. No need to play those notes. Just play a halftone down or up or better still play F# an octave up — who except for the composer will know the difference? (If you're having trouble following this, just ask a friend who has a piano to run through it with you.)

But far too many actors are unsure of the exact note that frightens them. They do know that they are approaching something dangerous and, in self-defense, they stop well before they get to it. When they do, they avoid not only the dangerous note but many, many notes on both sides of that note. This is unacceptable. It shortens the keyboard too radically and takes away many usable notes that are needed to play important roles.

There is a further caveat, this one for teachers and some universities. I taught in universities for many years but retired about fifteen years ago when a new wave of thinking was on the rise. There was a movement to make "better people" of their actors — to impose norms of behavior and sometimes political points of view on the students. The acting studio is no place for this. We are in the business of producing performing artists. It is the art form *itself* that is of real value. If the artist is a "good" person, that's nice, but history has taught us that it is not a prerequisite for being a fine artist. The art *alone* needs to be the concern of the acting teacher. Either you find real value in the art of acting itself or you should move your skills elsewhere.

It is not part of an acting teacher's job to make better people — period.

THE USE OF SKILL CLASSES

Present tense is often best approached in the "skills" sections of theater schools, i.e., the voice and movement classes. This is true for several reasons. The first is that the body stores knowledge in a much different way than the mind. The body's knowledge is often simpler and more direct and is certainly less judgmental than that of the head.

When I was a kid my parents insisted that I learn how to play the accordion — don't ask me why. I did as I was told and learned how to play the maniacal thing then promptly put it aside before I was a teenager. Thirty years later I rented a studio apartment in New York City and found an accordion in the closet. I picked it up, unsnapped the bellows, slid my left hand through the strap to the buttons which the player can't even see. (Only a significant sadist would create an instrument that you can't even see the damned buttons!) But lo and behold my fingers, quite unbidden by my mind, began to play scales — G minor 7th scales, C# scales, you name it. I couldn't then, nor can I now, tell you the order of the unseeable buttons, but my fingers remembered their lessons — they maintained the knowledge. The body is like that. Completely without judgment or concern of repercussion, the body remembers. From childhood, the body remembers how to be Present.

Accessing Present tense through voice class — not text or speech class — is also viable. The breath itself contains truths, and both finding and feeling the breath in the body can often be a revelation for an actor.

The beauty of Present tense work in both voice and movement class is that they are by nature nonverbal. They don't use language to parse ideas, and hence are often able to deal with concepts like being Present in a nonthreatening way.

OTHER APPROACHES TO GETTING PRESENT

Sport can also get people Present. It is simply impossible to hit a baseball traveling in excess of ninety miles an hour unless the batter is Present.

So can old record players. If you have an old record player, a good one, you can use it to momentarily get you Present. Put on a record with a song that really "gets you going" and you keep playing it until the effect pales. Then increase the volume to get back that feeling again. When that fails, slowly increase the speed of the turntable (I said a good one) and you'll get that feeling again momentarily. In each case your system is momentarily kicking into Present tense. (As an aside, it's pretty interesting to listen to music on a record player after all the years of hearing music digitally — it's deeper, richer, fuller and more fluid on the record player than on Spotify. Digital music is highly compressed. It's not compressed on the record and it's the reason that record sales are increasing.)

Traditionally, acting teachers have directed students toward moments of violence and sexuality in their lives to illustrate the concept of being Present. In theory, this makes sense but in practice it is proving to be contentious. Needless to say, the acting studio is not immune to the movements of social justice in the outside world. Adapting to the new realities while still remaining faithful to the job of producing emotionally connected artists is getting more and more complicated. Once again, if you don't believe the art has intrinsic value then you shouldn't be teaching it.

Because it is an actor's job to get Present, often in challenging situations, most production people forgive actors for involving themselves in what is normally considered just plain whacked-out behavior. They know that an actor who sits in their trailer with headphones on and the music cranked up so loud that the people in the next block can hear the lyrics is often just trying to get Present. So is the one who dances for hours on end before performing. Unfortunately, so is the actor involved in seriously self-destructive behavior. But getting Present, even under complex circumstances, is central to the job.

To illustrate: It's cold in Toronto in February. Not true. It's bone-numbing freezing. Yet, almost every year, some American or European production company forgets the vagaries of our winter and schedules outdoor scenes — sometimes with the actors in shorts — in February. It is not uncommon to see dozens of hapless technicians with portable hair dryers blowing the snow off the trees.

When they do finally shoot the scene, right before "action" is called, the actor is ordered to open their mouth. Crushed ice is tossed in. They are then instructed to chew, then spit. Upon "spit" the director calls, "Action." When the actor speaks, because they cooled down their mouths with the ice, they don't "blow smoke" into the frigid air.

Getting Present in such adverse circumstances is an actor's job and it is, to be frank, a significant achievement.

TO SUM UP:

1. Actors need to get Present.
2. Being Present is not natural and takes practice.
3. It is the work of teachers working with beginning actors.
4. How an actor achieves Present tense is their own business.
5. Being Present is what brings an actor out of the fog, wakes them up and makes them worthy of an audience's attention. Without being Present, there is no acting.
6. It is best taught in voice and movement class, but remains an uncomfortable fit with many universities.
7. The body remembers being Present.
8. The acting studio is no place for making "better people."

CHAPTER 2

The Principles

An actor's world has changed drastically from the time of Robert Lewis's fun to read 1958 book, *Method — or Madness?*. In that book Mr. Lewis references moments when a stage actor does an extraordinary thing with a pinky finger while lifting a cup of tea during the third act of a play. Well, we no longer have plays in three acts, and no one but no one is capable in a theater of seeing any actor's hand let alone their pinky do much of anything. Television has altered our very sight.

In Toronto we have street signs that were put up in the '50s. They were the appropriate size for the time. Apparently, the idea was to find a size that a person with average vision could read from thirty yards away traveling at thirty miles an hour. No one can read them now, even standing still, from ten yards away. The newer street signs around the city are six times bigger than the old ones and white on green or blue, not black on white, and they seem to holler "HEY BUDDY, THIS IS YOUR STREET." If they didn't no one would be able to read them. Thank television for this. God only knows what the cell phone is doing to our ability to see.

Further, some hour-long television shows are being shot on seven- or even six-day shooting schedules (rather than twelve or fourteen). And, many are block shot sometimes with different directors for each episode. These two facts alone change everything for an actor on television and film sets. As well, professional theater is now often given two and a half weeks for rehearsal, not four or even more, which was common in the early 2000s. These new realities require that an actor have a depth of understanding of their art that was not always necessary before.

The changes force actors to know the principles.

So, here they are:

1. Professional actors must be able to direct themselves.
2. It is an actor's job to be compelling, not necessarily right.
3. Modern acting is principally about selecting, not about pretending.
4. There is very seldom a neutral mask for the performer.
5. The Icon and the Action tell an actor what the scene is about, not the word.
6. Modern acting is almost exclusively performed in naturalism not realism.

The chapters that follow deal with each of these principles in depth. Remember, though, no technique of any sort works *unless you are Present first*, and you should resort to technique when you are lost — not when you are found — *or* when your work needs to become more compelling.

Most chapters conclude with a bullet point review of what has been covered. The appendix contains exercises. Some may prove helpful for those who are unfamiliar with this method of working.

CHAPTER 3

Principle #1 —
Actors Must Be Able to Direct Themselves

Chapter two was sorta simple, no? However, memorizing principles and applying them are two completely different things. Now we move on to application and, hey, big surprise, it gets a bit more complicated.

A professional actor should have some sort of system to allow them to assess the work that they see. It is not good enough to say, "Hey, I really liked that performance," or the vastly more common comment, "Hated it. Just hated it." Fine. Love a performance or hate it, I couldn't care less. What I care about is that you know why you are responding in the way you are responding. Actors have to have a language to analyze what they are seeing in another person's performance so they can apply it to their own work. The language you were taught at theater school simply is not accurate enough to be of real assistance. It didn't really analyze performance at all, it analyzed text. It was most often taught by directors whose sotto voce agenda was to make you easy to direct. That has nothing to do with acting well.

So here we go:

To know how to direct oneself an actor has to have a clear idea what makes up a moment of acting. You can't fix something if you don't know what component is broken or missing or incorrect or simply not very compelling.

Assuming that you are Present (always the first thing to check) then the problem, or glory, with any acting moment must exist in one of three areas: a) State of Being, b) the playing of Action or c) the opening of Images — all of which we'll examine further.

Because that's all that actors do: they *sit* in States of Being from which they *play* metaphoric Actions often by the *use* of Images both literal and physical.

In chart form it simplifies to this:

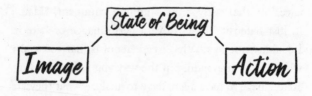

That's it: State of Being, Action and Image. There's nothing more with which to tinker.

States of Being determine the final product of a moment the same way that the left hand on the piano determines the key in which the melody is heard. Even a slight variation in a pianist's left hand totally changes the "meaning" of the music (sometimes from minor to major or the other way around). So it is for States of Being.

One actor finally twigged to this idea by saying to me, "It's like having a hangover, right?"

I recall doing one of those hesitations that all teachers know well. "Explain," I said.

"It's like you try to convince the girl in the Chinese takeout to give you one more piece of lemon chicken?"

I thought, "Convincing the girl to give you more lemon chicken is the playing of an Action, not a State of Being," but fortunately I kept my mouth shut.

"Yeah, David, it's one thing to ask for the extra chicken if you've just been cast in a great role, but it's a completely different idea if you have a terrible hangover and really hate everyone and everything because you feel so awful, and you have to convince this girl to give you an extra piece of chicken."

I smiled and agreed. The functional Action (more on function vs metaphoric actions later) of convincing the girl to give you an extra piece of chicken is the same in both scenarios, but the moment is completely different because you are in two different States of Being. *States of Being are the biggest controller of what a moment looks like.*

In the chicken example neither of the States of Being are Primaries (much more about that later), but they certainly influence the playing of the moment. It is important to note that the two different States of Being the "I just got cast in a great role" and the "I have a hangover" are completely independent of the Action.

Which leads us to the issue of separation of Action and State of Being. But let's deal with States of Being first in the next chapter.

I'll address the issues of Action and Image in separate chapters — so let's call the next chapter States of Being.

TO SUM UP:

1. Actors only get to tinker with Action/States of Being/Image to perform.
2. States of Being are the biggest of the controllers of what a moment looks like.
3. You *sit* in States of Being, from which you *play* Actions by the *use* of Images.

CHAPTER 4

States of Being

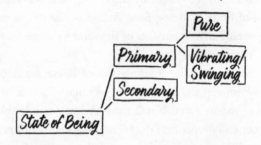

A State of Being is the emotional reality in which an actor begins a scene. That which is roiling inside an actor before a single word is spoken. It is, to a degree — but only a degree — analogous to Stanislavski's idea of given circumstances. If you've been trained in that methodology take a look at this new way of thinking. Don't try to translate back to what you know just yet. As I mentioned before, I never remove any system from an actor that is working for them. But adding to your kitbag is always of value.

A professional actor works from States of Being rather than given circumstances because the given circumstances are often outside the life experience of the actor — or any human being (see: Marvel films). State of

Being work allows actors to access that which they know well and looks beneath the text. Also, State of Being work is much more mobile and variable than given circumstances. State of Being work also avoids the desire to be right and therefore follows the second principle: an actor's job is to be *compelling* not necessarily *right*.

States of Being are also independent of the playing of Actions and can be generated on their own in order to create "most eloquent music." In fact, the separation of State of Being from Action is one of the most important artistic pursuits of the actor — more on that in chapter eight.

So here are the basics: States of Being are divided into Primaries and Secondaries. A Primary State of Being is an insatiate form. It will not burn itself out. It spirals deeper and deeper into the human heart without finding an ending. Secondary States of Being, although sometimes volatile, are finite and will pass of their own accord. Only when sitting in Primary States of Being is the old theater saw that "less is more" true. We've all worked with actors who hardly give off any signal then "hone" their performance. If they were sitting in Secondary States of Being, they go from little signal to almost none. The work does not become more interesting, it becomes smaller. The Secondary State of Being of I AM ANGRY when "honed" simply becomes less angry. While sitting in the Primary State of Being of I AM BETRAYED, when you show us less — it becomes deeper, i.e., more profoundly betrayed.

Finding, opening and sitting in Primary States of Being is an important part of an actor's art.

SOME REALITIES OF PRIMARY STATES OF BEING

When sitting in Primary States of Being that little voice in your head that links you to your sense of personal safety will attempt to talk you out of being in the Primary. In Primary States of Being you will find rehearsal whips by. In Primary States of Being the line between laughing and crying becomes blurred. In Primary States of Being you will feel fully alive, beautiful, tall, smart, clear skinned — name your favorite.

To see some examples go to proactorslab.com. You'll find two videos on the home page: the young girl with her kitten and Rayna in the Paul Simon video. Watch them. Both the little girl and Rayna are in the Right-Handed (which is to say positive, rather than negative) Primary State of Being of *I SEE I LOVE*.

Now open "Tribute to Leonard Cohen." In the concert k.d. lang sings "Hallelujah" — she is in the pure Right-Handed (positive) Primary State of Being of I AM ASCENDING. Later in the same concert Damien Rice sings "Famous Blue Raincoat" — he's sitting in the Left-Handed (negative) Primary State of Being of I AM FALLING.

Listen to both then come back to the book once again.

The idea of Primary and Secondary States of Being is mine and forms some of the base of my teaching at Pro Actors Lab. Here's where my thinking about this began. When I first returned to Toronto, I was sitting in a bar trying to complete a writing assignment that was already badly overdue. It's what I used to do when I lived in New

York City. When I was stuck for ideas, I'd just go to a bar and allow the faces there to inspire me. But the faces in this particular Toronto bar were dull, lifeless. Then an officious Flemish lady appeared on the bar's television and announced to the world — and in this case specifically to Canada — that our national hero, Ben Johnson, was going to be stripped of his gold medal in the Olympic 100-meter dash. Instantly, every face in the bar became fascinating as they all fell into the pure (as opposed to vibrating/swinging — more on this later too), Left-Hand (negative) Primary of I AM BETRAYED. The faces stayed glorious for about six seconds then returned to their dullness as they backed out of their facial bones and shifted from the Primary State of Being of I AM BETRAYED and into the Secondary State of Being of (the liberal one) I UNDERSTAND THAT IT'S HARD FOR A BLACK MAN IN CANADA or the (redneck one) I AM ANGRY THAT WE LET HIM INTO OUR COUNTRY AND LOOK WHAT HE DID. In both of these cases, either the liberal or the redneck, they are Secondaries and will burn themselves out — they disappear over time. The Primary State of Being of I AM BETRAYED does not. It goes on and on and on. I AM BETRAYED is too painful for most civilians to maintain — it is part of the reason that actors serve a real purpose in the universe. They do not roll the Primary State of Being of I AM BETRAYED into the Secondary of I AM ANGRY but rather allow us to view it from the safety of our living rooms.

Self-help books are filled with advice to those who find themselves inadvertently stuck in the Primary of I AM BETRAYED. "It wasn't your fault. It was his/her fault. Blame him/her." In other words, leave the Primary of I AM BETRAYED by "blaming him/her" which will allow you to enter the Secondary State of Being of I AM ANGRY — which will, unlike the Primary of I AM BETRAYED — burn itself out.

Here is a list of some Primary States of Being:

Left-Handed Pure Primaries (negative)

- I AM FALLING
- I AM BETRAYED
- I HAVE BETRAYED
- I AM LOST
- I BLEED INSIDE
- I AM IN PAIN
- I HAVE LOST MY FAITH
- I AM ALONE
- I SCREAM IN MY DREAMS
- OTHERS ARE ALIVE BUT I ONLY BREATHE IN AND OUT
- I AM IN TERROR
- I AM UGLY
- I SEE I LOATHE
- J'AI LA NAUSÉ
- I AM SICK
- I AM FAT
- I AM STUPID

- I AM IMPOTENT
- I AM UNTALENTED
- ANY "I CAN'T"

Right-Handed Pure Primaries (positive)

- I AM ASCENDING
- GOD IS IN HIS/HER/ITS HEAVEN AND ALL IS WELL IN THE WORLD
- I AM WORTHY (WORTH LISTENING TO, TOUCHING, KNOWING, SEEING, LOVING, ETC.)
- I REALLY SEE IT NOW, I HEAR IT ALL NOW
- I AM FULLY AWAKE
- I AM LOVED BY MY FATHER
- I AM LOVED BY MY MOTHER
- I SEE I LOVE
- I AM TRANSCENDING
- I AM GROWING AT LAST
- I AM IN AWE
- THEY RESPECT ME
- I AM NOT ALONE
- I AM BECOMING
- I AM ALIVE
- I AM POWERFUL
- I AM HERE, REALLY HERE

It is an actor's job to find, open and sit in Primary States of Being. It makes work more compelling. It gives the actor the right to stand in the light while others watch from the dark.

You want to act better? Fine, open and sit in Primary *not* Secondary States of Being. You will, by the by, be significantly more difficult to direct when you find and open them, but you will act better.

SWINGING

I have two children. Well, my wife and I have two children, and both have always been terrific athletes. When we walked them past a park, the kids would race into the playground and both would fall into the pure Right-Handed Primary of I SEE I LOVE because kids love things that they are good at and both were very good at the skills a playground offered. However, my son is older than my daughter, and by age six his running into the playground changed. Although my daughter was glorious to watch in her pure Right-Handed Primary of I SEE I LOVE, my son was fascinating to watch as he started in I SEE I LOVE, then believed himself to be too old for this kind of fun and vibrated (swung) between I SEE I LOVE and I KNOW I SHOULDN'T.

It is many people's reaction to chocolate cake, cigarettes, scantily clad members of the opposite or your own sex — pick your poison.

Sitting in pure Primaries has a tendency to make a person seem younger. In the film *Fargo* William H. Macy sits in pure Primaries. It's what makes him "flee the interview," park his Cadillac facing the highway right outside the motel in which he's trying to hide, to kick his little feet when he is caught and carried to the police car. He sits in the pure Left-Handed Primary of I AM ALONE. It drives his age down. To keep your age up in I AM ALONE you need to match it with AND I KNOW I DON'T HAVE TO BE. And to answer the question before it arises: no, I'm not talking about sitting one moment in I AM ALONE and then the next in I KNOW I DON'T HAVE TO BE. Just as in real life *both* States of Being are alive in your system at the same time. It's called Swinging.

For example, many people even as they are walking down the aisle to get married experience "Thank God, no more dating" *and* "Oh my God, no more dating!" at the same time. I was a smoker until my thirtieth birthday, and I knew perfectly well how bad cigarettes were for my health, but I loved cigarettes and almost everything about them. So I knew it was bad for me at the *same time* as I loved them. As an aside, it was reported to me that I was a wee bit terse in rehearsal for the show I directed right after I gave up the deadly weed.

I AM ALONE is a Primary that many people experienced in their childhood. When a young boy is having trouble learning to read and his parents insist that he have a tutor come over to the house and the boy runs away he is in I AM ALONE, and it is terrifying to watch because there is no swing, just terror.

STATES OF BEING — RIGHT VS LEFT

Most actors find getting to Left-Handed Primaries easier than getting to right-handed ones. In either instance Primaries must be Keyed (see chapter seven). As actors get more experienced, they realize that they need to play most Actions on the right and sit in States of Being on the left and vice versa. By doing that the audience is forced to take in more information at once, which is by its nature more interesting — especially if the information sits in a *dynamic juxtaposition*. It is an important method of making work more compelling.

Musicians do this by placing silence next to sound, dancers by placing movement next to stillness and writers by making you consider two independent events as if there is a causal relationship between them. Here is an example from James Lee Burke's fine novel *The Neon Rain*:

> Three years ago a small plane with a family on board from Tampa hit a bad headwind over the Gulf, used up all its gas, and pancaked into the lake ten miles out. They got out with only one life preserver. Both the father and mother were strong swimmers and could have struck out for the shore or the causeway, but they stayed with their three children and kept them afloat for two days. One by one the parents and the two oldest children slipped under the waves. The smallest child survived because his father had strapped him in the

life preserver and tied his shirt around the child's head to protect it from the sun.

Some miles to the west and just south of Morgan City was the crushed and barnacle-encrusted hull of a German U-boat that an American destroyer had nailed in 1942, when Nazi submarines used to lie in wait for the oil tankers that sailed from the refineries in Baton Rouge and New Orleans. Shrimpers in New Iberia told stories of the orange fires that burned on the southern horizon late at night, and of the charred bodies they pulled up in their nets. I didn't understand then who the Nazis were, but I imagined them as dark-uniformed slit-eyed creatures who lived beneath the water and who could burn and murder people of goodwill whenever they wished.

Years later, when I was in college, I dove down to that wreck with an air tank and a weight belt. It was in sixty feet of water, lying on its side, the deck railing and forward gun shaggy with moss, the painted identification numbers still visible on the conning tower. The stern was tilted downward into deeper water, and I thought I could see the frenetic, turning movements of sand sharks near the screws. My heart was clicking in my chest, I was breathing oxygen rapidly from my tank, and actually sweating inside my mask. I determined that I wasn't going to be overcome by my childhood fears, and I swam down to the dark, massive outline of the conning tower and knocked against the steel plate with the butt of my bowie knife.

Then the strangest occurrence of my life took place as I hovered above the wreck. I felt a cold current blow across me, a surge from the darkness beyond the submarine's screws, and air bubbles rose from under the hull. I heard the metal plates start to grate against the bottom, then there was a crunching, sliding sound, a dirty cloud of moss and floating sand, and suddenly the sub trembled almost erect and began sliding backwards off the continental shelf. I watched it, horrified, until it disappeared in the blackness. The sand sharks turned like brown minnows in its invisible wake.

I learned that this particular wreck moved several miles up and down the Louisiana coastline, and it was only coincidence that its weight had shifted in a strong current while I was on top of it. But I could not get out of my mind the image of those drowned Nazis still sailing the earth after all these years, their eye sockets and skeletal mouths streaming seaweed, their diabolical plan still at work under the Gulf's tranquil, emerald surface.

A navy destroyer broke the spine of their ship with depth charges in 1942. But I believed that the evil they represented was held in check by the family who sacrificed their lives so their youngest member could live (pages 207–209).

What James Lee Burke does so compellingly is make the reader consider the possibility of a cause and effect relationship between the drowned family and the Nazi submarine. It makes the totality much, much greater than the sum of the two individual stories. So that one plus one equals three or more, if you will.

For actors compelling juxtaposition can be achieved by sitting in a State of Being on the left while playing an Action on the right or, obviously, vice versa. Once again, making one plus one equal three or more.

THE SPECIAL PLACE OF I AM FALLING

I AM FALLING is a particularly important State of Being. It sits far on the left hand (although there is the Alice in Wonderland I AM FALLING, which is the one full of awe and wonder which sits on the right hand).

The basic acting "dropping in" exercise practiced in so many theater schools is a form of falling to yourself. Running by its nature is a series of falls and catches — that is what differentiates it from walking.

More importantly Falling is the central concern of much of Western literature. It is no mistake that we in the Judeo-Christian tradition live "after the fall" and that we "fall in love" and "fall apart." Here is James Joyce's extraordinary passage on falling that concludes his short story collection *Dubliners*.

A few light taps upon the pane made him turn to the window. It had begun to snow again. He watched sleepily the flakes, silver and dark, falling obliquely against the lamplight. The time had come for him to set out on his journey westward. Yes, the newspapers were right: snow was general all over Ireland. It was falling on every part of the dark central plain, on the treeless hills, falling softly upon the Bog of Allen and, farther westward, softly falling into the dark mutinous Shannon waves. It was falling, too, upon every part of the lonely churchyard on the hill where Michael Furey lay buried. It lay thickly drifted on the crooked crosses and headstones, on the spears of the little gate, on the barren thorns. His soul swooned slowly as he heard the snow falling faintly through the universe and faintly falling, like the descent of their last end, upon all the living and the dead.

TO SUM UP:

1. The difference between Primary vs Secondary States of Being
2. Swinging Primary vs pure Primary
3. The division of Right-Handed vs Left-Handed States of Being
4. Four videos to watch on proactorslab.com

5. Using vibrating/swinging Primaries to keep age up
6. Using pure Primaries to drop age
7. The fact that Leading actors almost always sit in vibrating/swinging Primaries
8. The use of Right-Handed Primaries against Left-Handed Actions and vice versa
9. Compelling juxtaposition to make the work more compelling
10. The special place of I AM FALLING
11. If you haven't read James Joyce's *Dubliners*, you have a treat ahead of you

CHAPTER 5

The Playing of Actions

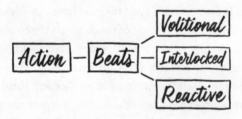

Acting is quintessentially the playing of Actions. Nothing that an actor does is independent of the attempt to accomplish something — i.e., play an Action. The paradigm for the playing of an Action is always the same. It is: If I had the right to *determine* the end of the scene, what would my acting partner do at the end of the scene? And that paradigm for the modern actor never changes, from acting in *Gammer Gurton's Needle* to any moment in *Jojo Rabbit*, it is always the same.

The playing of Actions put an end to the Victorian style of declarative performance that gave the world Edward Kean and John Wilkes Booth (for that matter).

It is this style of acting that is mocked in *Long Day's Journey into Night*. The father's endless performances of *The Count of Monte Cristo* no doubt left no piece of furniture unmunched. It was this kind of acting that the method ideas, coming first out of Russia and later out of New York City, put an end to.

The requirement that actors play Actions at all times began the modern age of acting.

The basic confabulation of playing an Action is that you have a problem that only your acting partner can solve. If the writing is good they too have a problem only you can solve. The playing of the Action is the convincing of your acting partner to solve your problem without you having to solve theirs. How do we do this? We pursue an Action. How do we pursue an Action? Read your acting partner's vulnerabilities (see chapter thirteen), play to those vulnerabilities and hide the fact that you are playing an Action (anyone who knows they are being manipulated will stop you from manipulating them; if they don't they are a stupid character and audiences do not follow stupid characters) and commit fully to winning your Action.

It becomes the obvious problem with most of the productions of *Othello*. If Iago is so easily able to trick Othello, then Othello is not bright enough to be worthy of our attention. It's why good productions of the play pay close attention to making Othello smart and Iago devious enough that he could have tricked you or me. No mustache twirling Iago's please!

There are two forms of Action. One is literal (sometimes referred to as functional), such as asking someone to marry you. Asking them to marry you is the function — the plot. But the playable metaphor for the actor is: I'm trying to change my life. The literal is part of the plot and is the director's territory, but it's not what an actor plays. An actor plays the metaphoric.

It's only seldom that the plot action (the literal one) is something that the actor knows all that much about but the metaphor behind the literal always gives actors access to their own resources. For example: the scene has you telling your brother that he's about to marry a terrible person. Say you have no brother. Say you've never even come near having to do something like this. Fine. But you have probably participated in the metaphor: to open the eyes of a friend. Everything from telling a five-foot-one-inch guy that it's unlikely the Raptors will be interested in his remarkable dribbling skills, to trying to get an addicted friend to see what they are doing to themself and others. TO OPEN THE EYES OF A FRIEND is a playable metaphoric Action that allows the actor to draw from their own deep life knowledge. This adds weight (ballast) to the specifics of the scene of telling your brother he's about to marry a devious person.

At its base, an Action is an effort to change a person's mind.

Years ago, my wife worked for the Canada/USSR business council and was often away from the house for a few weeks at a time. Well, we had a rule in the house: two cookies per day. Beth, my daughter, was about four or five, and she'd eaten two cookies by about seven a.m. Then she began to play an Action against me: "I'll be your best friend," she said, to which I smiled and said, "No more cookies." Then she said, "I'll make you breakfast," to which I said, "No more cookies." Then she paused because she'd run out of tactics (volitional beats, see below) and she cut directly to the Action itself and said, "Change your mind!" Which is the playable metaphor behind the literal Action of to get another cookie.

Then you have to attach the action to a Driver. Oops, Drivers — we'll get to those later.

Back to Actions. In all naturalistic plays (all TV and film with truly rare exception are naturalistic) you commit to succeeding at your Action before you even open your mouth. The Action is propelled by some problem that you have.

Actions can be divided into beats. If you went to theater school they probably taught you how to use transitive verbs — verbs that act upon something, as in "hit" in the line: "I hit Bob with all my might." Hit is a transitive verb because it has an object — in this case Bob. Intransitive verbs, such as "to make" or "to do," don't take an object and are not actable.

Theater schools — especially undergraduate programs where they need to grade students and hence need materials to justify grades — love to make actors write out beat play, putting a transitive verb beside each unit or beat. But there are problems — obvious problems — with this approach because there are three kinds of beats: volitional beats (the ones they taught you in theater school and that I refer to as tactics), interlocked beats (where you are not trying to achieve anything because you are on defense) and reactive beats.

It's easiest to illustrate it this way: two-person hockey but only one puck. If you have the puck you have *volition* (you can achieve your Action); if you don't have the puck you can't achieve your Action — all you can do is try to stop your acting partner from achieving their Action. If they move right, you counter by moving left and vice versa. You are in *interlock* with your acting partner. But, if the puck deflects off your stick and breaks your nose and your line is "Fuck, fuck, fuck!" you are not playing an Action at all. You are in *reactive*. In *Twelfth Night* Viola is in reactive in act five when she sees her brother who she thought had drowned at sea. She gives a lovely speech, but she is not trying to do anything to anyone, she is just emotionally vomiting — she's in reactive. Acting becomes most compelling when actors are in reactive. Hence, talented actors dictate to characters (in order to find reactive moments) rather than letting characters dictate to them. Actors dictate to characters (while staying within the *HIT* parameters — see chapter thirteen) because the main job of a professional actor is to be compelling, not necessarily right — more on that later.

Besides, professional actors seldom break scripts down into beats for a very obvious reason. If you do this you are assuming that you know how your acting partner is going to play their moments. If your line is "I love you, Clarice," and you assume you can put the verb "to caress" beside your line. That's fine if Clarice behaves the way you think she should, but if the actor playing Clarice decides to put her finger up her nose and pull out the contents therein then you playing "to caress" on your line makes no sense because Clarice has taken you out of volition and put you into interlock by what she has chosen to do.

As a quick note about working on set: if the director doesn't stop Clarice from picking her nose, then you have to react to that. It's not your job to re-direct other actors — it's the director's job. If your fellow actor does something that stops you from getting to your next line, then whether you cause a fuss depends on where you are on the call sheet and the politics of the set.

Actors on set do have a tendency to use beat breakdown when they are playing opposite kids, animals or civilians. And it makes sense to do so since it's pretty unlikely that you are going to get any accurate signal from such acting partners. As well, as the pro you are expected to lead the scene.

But on the whole, professional actors don't bother with beat breakdown. They commit to achieving their Action and then deal with whatever comes out of their acting partner. It's one of the things American actors find very difficult when they work in the U.K. British actors like to rehearse solidifying how a scene is to be played, while most Americans value the immediacy that happens when you don't know what happens next.

The thing that is thrilling about good American style

acting is that it's *really happening* right in front of you, and to manage this you have to get Present, commit to the playing of the Action, then one, two, three — GO!

DREAM ACTIONS BIG!

It is important as it's almost always wrong to play a scene in order "to get a hug" or "to clear up" something. Actions are bigger than that because they propel the drama. Often Actions are unaccomplishable. And they should be. Here's a prosaic example. Some men when trying to break up relationships with women play this Action: if I had the right to determine the end of the scene she would say, "You're right. How brave of you. I'll always have a special place in my heart for you. And how's about one for the road."

Well he may come in with that Action but what probably happens is that he mentions distance, she screams, he relents and they go out for dinner.

Just because you dream Actions big doesn't mean that you succeed at them, but dream Actions big — no "to get a hug" nonsense.

THE PROBLEM WITH BEAT PLAYING ACTORS

Actors who use beats exclusively (as opposed to committing to Actions) come off as control freaks or villains. Stage actors are often seen that way in TV and film, since stage acting needs to be solidified by beats so the performance can be repeated eight times a week.

Television and film actors need to "get there" about one and a half times, then you move on.

SUPER OBJECTIVES

In well-thought-through scripts (think film rather than most series TV) an actor can spot a moment of climax and attach a Super Objective to that moment. With that, the whole film from the actor's point of view *drifts* either toward or away from the moment of climax. It puts up guide rails so that the actor doesn't end up exploring everything and everyone during the course of the work.

Often Super Objectives are unaccomplishable. And they should be. Hamlet actually tries to find and settle the hidden rot in an entire country — talk about a big Super Objective! Of course, the play is also five-plus hours long.

Here's a Super Objective that lasts over many, many seasons of a show: SEEKING HOME. The leading character in *The Wire*, McNulty, whether he knows it or not, is seeking a place to call home. All around him others, even criminals, at least have something to call their own. He does not (a very good reason to cast a British actor in an American setting). Here's the very first scene from the five seasons of that brilliant show.

```
THE WIRE, Sı. Eı, First scene:

EXT. STREET CORNER — NIGHT

A dead body lies in the street,
with a bullet hole and massive
bloodstain in his back. Police and
forensic investigators are all around
collecting evidence. Children are
```

                sitting on the stoops of neighboring
                houses watching everything as if
                it's a TV show. Jimmy McNulty is
                questioning a witness who was friends
                with the victim.

                          MCNULTY
                So your boy's name is what?

                          FRIEND
                Snot

                          MCNULTY
                You called the guy Snot?

                          FRIEND
                Snotboogie, yeah.

                          MCNULTY
                "Snotboogie." He like the name?

                          FRIEND
                What?

                          MCNULTY
                Snotboogie.

                The friend simply shrugs his shoulders
                to say he didn't know.

                          MCNULTY (CONT'D)
                And this kid whose mama went to
                the trouble of christening him
                Omar Isaiah Betts? You know,
                he forgets his jacket, so his
                nose starts running, and some
                asshole, instead of giving him a
                Kleenex he called him "Snot." So

he's "Snot" forever. It doesn't
seem fair.

                    FRIEND
          Life just be that way, I guess.

                    MCNULTY
          So. Who shot Snot?

                    FRIEND
          I ain't going to no court!

The friend takes a long pause.

                    FRIEND (CONT'D)
          Motherfucker didn't have to put
          no cap in him though.

                    MCNULTY
          Definitely not.

                    FRIEND
          I mean he coulda just whipped
          his ass, like we always whip
          his ass.

                    MCNULTY
          I agree with you.

                    FRIEND
          He gon' kill Snot. Snot being
          doing the same shit since I
          don't know how long. Kill a man
          over some bullshit. I'm saying,
          every Friday night in an alley
          behind the cut-rate, we rolling
          bones, you know? I mean all the

boys from around the way, and we
roll till late.

                    MCNULTY
An alley crap game, right?

                    FRIEND
And like every time, Snot, he'd
fade a few shooters. Play it
out till the pot's deep. Then
he'd snatch and run.

                    MCNULTY
What, every time?

                    FRIEND
Couldn't help hisself.

                    MCNULTY
Let me understand you. Every
Friday night you and your boys
would shoot crap right? But
every Friday night your pal
Snotboogie, he'd wait til there
was cash on the ground, then
grab the money and run away?

The friend nods in the affirmative

                    MCNULTY (CONT'D)
You let him do that?

                    FRIEND
We'd catch him and beat his
ass, but ain't nobody ever go
past that.

> MCNULTY
> I gotta ask ya. If every time
> Snotboogie would grab the money
> and run away, why'd you even
> let him in the game?

> FRIEND
> What?

> MCNULTY
> If Snotboogie always stole the
> money, why'd you let him play?

> FRIEND
> Got to. . . This America, man.

The friend has America — McNulty has nothing. The search for something to call your own/to call home is the *Ulysses* search, vast, complicated and unending — and profoundly human. It has been an important part of humanity's thinking for thousands of years. It is the classic Super Objective of a long series.

Which brings us to Drivers.

DRIVERS

These ideas started with my reading of Irwin Yalom's book *Love's Executioner*.

Drivers are what propels an Action. They answer the question "how much do I want to succeed at my Action?" You can only enter violence if the Driver is very high, imminent.

Some actors are stake players. They artificially raise or lower the stakes of the playing of their Action. I've often found stake players to be too limited — it's as if they have a five-speed car and slam the thing from first to fourth then back to second. It's too unrefined a method since the answer to "how much do you want to win your Action?" has several hundred gradations.

Hence, I resort to Drivers.

The ideas for this, as mentioned above, come from a Jungian psychologist, Irwin Yalom, who suggests that human behavior is controlled basically by five Drivers, all of which are fears.

Here they are:

- The fear that I am not worthy of being loved (I am stupid, I am fat, I am ugly, etc.) It's the one that most actors use.
- The fear that I will die alone and forgotten.
- For actors from a faith tradition, the fear that there is no order or reason in the universe, that randomness controls everything (i.e., there is no guiding force).
- The fear that those you love will die.
- And what I refer to as the Peer Gynt fear, the fear that you wasted your life (see Ibsen's *Peer Gynt* beginning of act five).

You only need to open up *one* of the fears — and by the way you'll be pretty impossible to be around while you work on it. These primal fears are dark, nasty places in the human heart. You have to open one so that you can contact it anytime you wish and attach it to the playing of an Action — it answers the question "how much?"

So for example: I play a moment and the director calls cut. If they turn to me and ask, "This doesn't mean anything to you?" all that they are saying is that I am wearing the Driver too low. I allow the Driver to be more present, imminent, and play again. If they call cut and say, "Over the top." Fine, all they are saying is that the Driver is now too present. I pull it back down a bit and play again. They allow me to finish the scene then turn to me and say, "See?"

And I think, "Ain't you the smarty pants."

Drivers allow an actor to give a director the external intensity that they want, but creating it all from inside.

SEQUENCING

The sequence in which an actor places States of Being/Actions/Images determines the kind of acting they will produce.

Stage actors (and correctly so) place Action first: the Action produces the State of Being (which duplicates a form of the Action and hence allows it to travel to the far reaches of the theater).

Classical stage actors begin with the Image (the word). The word generates the State of Being and the Action lags behind. In much of classical theater the Action is little more than "he hears me and it changes him."

Clearly this came from a time when people believed in the intrinsic power of the word, and just as clearly that is no longer true.

Film/TV actors place the State of Being first, then the Action and far behind the word.

POSTS

Posts are a directing idea that actors need to understand. Posts are the guiding mechanism for plot within the playing of Action (remembering that an Action only imposes on a scene not the whole script). These are moments where the vector of the plot needs to change. They are dictated by a good director, and I never advise actors to argue about posts. They secure the story for the director and the audience. However, how you get to and from a post is actor business and not director business. There are times when an actor really does have to insist to a director that "this is my territory not yours."

TO SUM UP:

1. Paradigm for playing of Action
2. Action playing as the death knell for Victorian acting
3. Drifts and Super Objectives
4. Actors dictate to characters to create reactive moments
5. The nature of interlocked beats as opposed to volitional ones

6. The primacy of reactive beats
7. Super Objectives
8. Posts
9. Dream actions big
10. The problem with beat players
11. List of five Drivers
12. Need to open a Driver
13. How to use them on set
14. The ordering of Image/Action/State of Being determines what kind of acting:
    a. State of Being to Action to Image = TV and Film Acting
    b. Action to State of Being to Image = Modern Stage Acting
    c. Image to State of Being to Action = Classical Stage Acting
15. Posts

CHAPTER 6

Images

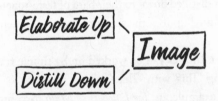

Image work is the third side of the triangle.

If you read a script and have no idea where to start, then do this — circle all the concrete Images (nouns) that you say. Then open each.

HOW TO OPEN IMAGES

You either *elaborate up* or *distill down* to open a noun so that it means exactly what it is. For example, if your line is "I opened the refrigerator and pulled out a can of Coke," you have to get "refrigerator" and "can of Coke" right. So asking what kind of refrigerator we are talking about is not a silly actor question, it's a request to be exact so that you can either elaborate it up (write about it, photograph it, sing it — whatever opens the Image for you) or distill it down to something you can either taste or touch or smell. As for the can of Coke, well, it's different than a can of Pepsi. Here I think it best to distill: What is the distinctive nature of the TASTE of Coke? Maybe the sharp sting of the first sip.

The problem gets more intense when you realize that "friendship" and "love" and "hate" are all Images and must be either distilled down to their base of taste/touch/smell or elaborated up to some specifics that make them open for you.

Some Images can be worked on by simple transfers. Replacing "This" with "That."

For example, in *The Duchess of Malfi*, two brothers, who are princes, believe their sister is pregnant from having an affair with a servant. At the time it was believed that pregnant women couldn't eat apricots without puking, so the brothers trick her into eating apricots — and she upchucks. Personally, I find apricots a rather innocuous fruit, however, when I worked in Shanghai I was presented with some foodstuffs that I found quite puke-inducing. So, if I play the young woman who is pregnant and is presented with apricots, I direct transfer those apricots to the steamed turtle whose head was cut off and put on my plate in an after-show celebration.

Direct transfers are homework — like much of what we are talking about here in this chapter. Once you are on set — it's one, two, three, GO.

There are direct transfers for nouns and Keys and Transfers for people, places, States of Being, Actions, etc. — more on that in later chapters.

CLICHÉS

There is one more idea that is useful for some actors working on images. Unwind clichés and play their origins, not their present meanings. For example, "He was clutching at straws." The phrase simply means that he was desperate. But the origin is more interesting. The phrase "clutching at straws" comes from seventeenth-century sailing ships. When the ship sank and the mariners (almost all of whom could not swim) were in the water, the last thing that they thought could keep them afloat was the straw from the belly of the ship — hence the phrase "clutching at straws."

Use the origin if you can find it, and the meaning will pop.

TO SUM UP:

1. Open Images through distilling or elaborating.
2. Unwind clichés to find their original meanings.

CHAPTER 7

Tool #1 — Keying

There are several chapters in the book entitled "Tools." This is the first one. Tools are also inserted into other chapters as needed.

To be able to make some of the things in the previous chapter work an actor needs to have a memory recall system. There are only really two: one, Affective Memory, that made the Actors Studio in New York famous, and the other I teach called Keying.

Both begin the same way. Actors must be accurate with what they are trying to recall. You can recall a person, a place, a State of Being, an Action, an Image — anything that has produced a memory.

In Keying what you are doing is training the frontal lobe of your brain to trace the synapses (nerve linkages) back to the part of the brain that stores memory. It's helpful to think of that part of the brain as a black box that records everything you've ever felt, seen, said, etc.

With Affective Memory this is done by recreating the exact circumstances under which the event, feeling, etc., took place, hence, in theory allowing the actor to relive it. Well, I'm afraid I have three problems with this. Foremost is that as a student I couldn't do it. I would be surrounded by actors pulling out their hair while I felt — well, nothing, not unlike the famous lyric in *A Chorus Line*. I'm willing to put this down to a personal failure on my part, but my other two objections are not personal.

The first is extremely practical. Affective Memory takes time and every TV and film actor has experienced the moment on set when, as they walk toward camera setup, a PA approaches them with those flimsy, small pages — all of which have changes on them. In the revised scene you're talking to a female and not a male, now you're contemplating marriage not murder — well, you get the idea. And you have all of five minutes to both get the new lines down *and* find the emotional reality behind them. Affective Memory is just too slow a process for the hurried realities of working on series TV and many films.

My last objection is a bit more eccentric.

I can't get over the feeling that Affective Memory hurts some actors. I grant this is an outré point of view, but it's been my experience that too many times a talented actor goes down the rabbit hole of Affective Memory and either becomes enamored with the *reason* for the feeling or plunges so deeply into the feeling that they cannot harness it in aid of their acting. In the first case their interest in the *why* of feeling is antithetic to actually feeling — in the other, well, it can be damaging to the point that the actor can no longer gain enough control to be able to act at all.

So, needless to say, I don't teach Affective Memory, but if Affective Memory works for you, please go ahead and use it.

I teach what I call Keying. You can Key a person, a place, an event, a State of Being, an Action and many more things. Keying is an attempt to find the single thing (the Key) for the person, place, State of Being, etc., *and* you want the Key to be something you can taste, touch or smell. (If you are a real musician, I will include "or hear" — but only if you are a real musician.) Do note I don't include "see" in this list.

Here are some examples. Let's start with an easy one. I had a long and complicated relationship with my father. Trying to bring him up holus-bolus is impossible. But, I have a Key for him: the smell of Lucky Strike cigarettes. He was drafted in World War II and Lucky Strike supplied smokes to the soldiers. Although he stopped smoking by the time I was five, the memory of the distinctive smell of Luckies (LSMFT: Lucky Strike Means Fine Tobacco — who says advertising doesn't work!) stayed with me. If the line is "Yes, he was my father," I can get "father" accurately by smelling Lucky Strikes — eventually, with practice, I can get there by just thinking the words "Lucky Strike."

Another example. When I came back to Toronto after being gone for over twenty years I was driving home from my first meeting at York University (boy did they love meetings!) and I was listening to the Blue Jays game on the radio. And because I'd lived in New York all those years, I found it perfectly acceptable to yell at the radio when George Bell fucked up yet another fly ball in left field. But while I was yelling at the radio, I heard other people yelling at their radio. I looked to my left and there were four Sikh men, all in traditional dress, in a Volkswagen convertible shouting at George Bell.

This was clearly the State of Being I AM FALLING — the Right-Handed one (the Alice in Wonderland one). So, I did as I had trained myself to do and ran my right thumb along the inside of my steering wheel, picking up the distinctive feel of the leather strapping there. And instantaneously I AM FALLING on my right was locked in that feeling in my thumb.

Another — I directed a production of *Three Sisters* and I had a talented young actor playing Rode, the young soldier who loses everything in the fire scene. He has a famous speech where he lists exactly what he has lost in the conflagration. As we worked on it, it became clear that something was very wrong. He couldn't settle on a State of Being. Finally, after a very long day he asked if we could stay behind and work on it. Although it was against the rules, I agreed.

When everyone was gone, he turned to me and said "I want to play this in I AM FREE" — a pure Right-Handed Primary. I thought that was sorta neat, so I said, "Sure." We began. I made him speak loudly and fast, free-associating off the word "free." He started with night as opposed to day, then weekends as opposed to weekdays and he went on for a full five minutes. Then I stopped him and made him run hard for five minutes, and when he finished that, he started again free-associating from the word "free," speaking loudly and as quickly as he could. We alternated five minutes of talking, five of running until about a half hour into the process, he began to talk about the smell of gasoline. It came up over and over again, like a blip in a computer (thank you, Tom Stoppard and *The Real Thing*). I told him to stop and explain. And he did. It turned out that he came from a large working-class family in Winnipeg — thirteen kids — and he was the only boy! Yikes! And they had a cottage that they rented for two weeks every summer north of the city. And because he was the boy, he got to drive the motorboat. The smell of gasoline.

For him it was the Key to the State of Being of I AM FREE. It was also the Key for the complicated Right-Handed Primary I AM LOVED BY MY FATHER.

Another — the artistic director of a large regional theater in Middle America thought it was clever to hire me, the only Canadian director that he knew, to mount the quintessential American play *Ah, Wilderness!*. It's the one gentle Eugene O'Neill play. It culminates in a young boy getting his first kiss on a dock in the moonlight at the end of the summer.

So he wrote to me — yeah, we wrote back then — on this lovely rice paper that the theater used for formal correspondence. He offered me the play and asked me to come out to see this fifteen-year-old boy who he thought could play the role. So I got on a plane and flew out to meet the boy. And he was smart and had strong features and could repeat, so I agreed. Then the artistic director said, "I have this girl," to which I said, "No. I'll go back to New York and get an actress who can do the role." There were small-boned, short actresses in their late twenties who could pass onstage as teenagers. I got in touch with my favorite, and it turned out she was available and liked the play, so two weeks later, eleven New York actors, my late-twenty-something small-boned actress and I boarded a plane and flew to Middle America.

That very night we sat down to read the play, and it became obvious that this young local boy was very — I mean *very* — struck with my small-boned actress from New York. That being the case, every time we came to the kiss scene, we would work right up to the kiss then I would stop them and we would jump to just after the kiss.

We did this over and over again, then one day that scene was on its feet and as we approached the kiss the stage manager handed me one of those lovely pieces of rice paper and it said, "Your father called."

Well, it was the early '80s, calling long distance was unbelievably expensive and besides my father never called, so I was completely distracted. But my attention was yanked back to the present when I heard my New York actress shout, "David, David!"

They had done the kiss — and the boy had fainted dead away in her arms and she was holding him.

Well, it was a great moment — it was the first time in my life that I realized that I was no longer young. That I would never again feel the glory this young boy felt in kissing this girl. It's an incredibly complicated Left-Handed Primary State of Being that I can get by just saying the words "rice paper." Rice paper had nothing to do with the feeling, but it was the Key to the feeling. And I can access it any time I need it.

The whole process is called Keying and Transferring because you have to use the Key to open the feeling or whatever you're attempting to recall then Transfer it to the circumstances of the scene. It takes some practice but is a very powerful tool and one used by many actors especially for close-ups. It's invaluable when you have to do your coverage without an acting partner — which happens to many actors who are lower on the call sheet — or on Friday when everyone just wants to go home.

Actors collect Keys and use them to make the work more compelling.

This leads to the idea that actors should keep diaries. I'm of two minds about this — one part of me says that it's nothing more than a way of making an actor feel like they are doing the necessary work when in fact they are not. We have all played against an actor who writes a whole novel about their character but in fact says the lines exactly the same as they did on the first reading. On the other hand, if the diary is about the actor's life — what they felt, experienced, observed on a daily or weekly basis — it can be very useful *if* the actor goes back and rereads what they wrote, looking for Keys as in "Shit, when he said that to me, I felt this," and the name of "this" is —— and the Key for that is ——. (Fill in the blanks.)

It's part of the way of staying an artist even when you aren't working. As I said before it is important that Tuesdays mustn't feel like Fridays, that November should not feel like April — artists must force themselves into Present tense — and allow themselves to see. My college roommate's brother runs a business out of Taos, New Mexico. And every day at noon he makes his workers stop what they are doing and go outside and look at the profound physical beauty of New Mexico. Although he is not a practicing artist, doing this is very much something actors should force themselves to do.

TRIGGERS

Triggers are not the same as Keys and Transfers, but they live in the same realm. A Trigger is a sound, a sight, a smell, a thing that triggers a virulent emotional response — almost always on the left. Actors collect these as well as Keys. I remember doing a workshop with a fabulously talented young actor (who passed away in the AIDS epidemic, like so many actors I'd worked with in New York) playing Hamlet. He was great in every scene except where he finds his mother languid in her bedchamber.

I was frightened that the scene brought up dragons for him on his emotional piano keyboard. But when I broached him about it, he told me that was not the problem. He said, "I need a springboard" to get emotionally into the scene.

As per usual with Triggers, the actor, not the director (in this case, me) came up with the solution. He asked the actress playing his mother to spit into a tissue and toss it on the floor before he entered. She did, he Triggered and it was volcanic.

In his mind, the damp tissue was Claudius's doing. He'd fucked Hamlet's mother then cleaned himself and thrown the tissue on the ground — the Trigger. We had to change the tissue to a handkerchief, since the play was staged vaguely in period, but it worked just the same.

Food can Trigger very strong Left-Handed States of Being — odor is another very valuable Trigger source.

A NOTE ON BEHAVIOR

There are several notes on behavior throughout this book but here's the first one.

You behave the way that you do in your life because of your family, your friends, your coworkers and perhaps your church. But this is *learned* behavior and is not really you. It is *not* the self from which we want to Key and Transfer. Your hidden self, the one you visit only in the darkness, is quintessentially you, and the one wherein your art lies. It is your ETHOS. (We will get to that in the chapter on auditioning.)

Actors make the mistake of drawing from their learned behavior, saying things like, "Well, when that happens to me —" My response as their director was always to stop them and remind them the response they were referencing was not experienced when they were in Present tense, and that the response they were referring to was from their learned behavior, not from their real self — their ethos.

TO SUM UP:

1. A note on Keying vs Affective Memory
2. Three objections to Affective Memory
3. Several examples of how Keying works
4. A note on behavior
5. An example of Triggering

CHAPTER 8

Principle #2 —
Be Compelling, Not Necessarily Right

When actors are dealing with a Tennessee Williams script, they need to offer respect to that text. That play has worked for fifty years. Besides, Mr. Williams killed himself to get the words as perfect as he could. If your production doesn't work — it's your fault, not the text's.

But professional actors seldom get to work on Tennessee Williams plays. They work on TV and film scripts which are by their nature all new, totally untested pieces. Offering them the same respect — respect usually leading to *trying to get it right* — as a Tennessee Williams script makes no sense. No one knows if there is a right way in a new script. So, all an actor can do is try to be compelling within the parameters of the script.

To be blunt: the object of professional actors is to be so damned interesting that someone in the London or the Tokyo or the Rome film industry sits up and says, "Who the hell is that — and who's his agent?"

It is the career building part of the business of this art form.

The actor is a member of a team while working on a specific project but must never be suckered by the idea that somehow the project is the be-all and end-all, that (here's my favorite) "we are all a family." Yeah, yeah, yeah except that the director or showrunner is always the parent and sometimes a parent leaves the family and doesn't bother taking the kids with them.

I'm not telling you to be a pain in the ass on set, but I'm telling you not to be just a function of the director's vision — or of the plot. Every time you shoot you should be aware that the audience you want to reach is in some film studio far away from the set, looking for someone just like you for their next project — if you can show them that you are a compelling artist.

WORKING WITH DIRECTORS

You have to get the director to direct *through* you, not on top of you, because you have real skin in this game. And that "skin" is different than the director's. Especially on television, the director's job is to get it in the can on time and to be sure the plot is clear. Your job is to make people in the audience wish they could meet you *or* be thrilled they'll never meet someone like you.

Your job and a director's job are often in conflict — and on set they often clash. Now that clash can be petty power struggles and stupid, or it can be the collision of creative minds that can lead to the betterment of the project. But the collision of creative minds can't happen if you're nothing more than one member of an ensemble.

Ensembles! Only a university could come up with

the idea of acting ensembles, i.e., giving all power over to the director.

A set is a place for strong but fair ideas (ideas that are based on real insight, not a desire to shine above others). There is good tension on set and bad tension on set. The former is about art. The latter is about power.

Young directors present another kind of problem. Directing on TV and film now requires a lot of technical skill. For a twenty-three-year-old to direct, they must have slept hugging their computer from age six — and gained their knowledge of the world from TV and maybe film. They often have very limited life or social skills. Because of that, too many young directors see only one way of shooting a scene (often a duplication of something they saw on TV). If their idea for the scene doesn't fit the actor they try to shove the actor into a mold even if that isn't right for the performer.

No actor can do every role or even one role dozens of different ways. Remember the joke in *A Midsummer Night's Dream* is that Bottom thinks he can play all the roles. Professional actors know what they can and cannot do — although trying something outside their comfort zone can at times, and with some sensitivity, be a good thing.

But a director having only one way to skin a cat is a recipe for disaster.

As Mark Twain said, "If a man wants to carry a cat home by the tail, I say let him. I don't think he'll ever try that again but it's not always easy to be eccentric." I grant that's not exactly on point, but I do love that quote.

When I lived in New York City I spent a lot of time with dancers. In some ways they were the only true artists since there wasn't a penny in their world — talk about doing something for love! And they would talk about forcing choreographers to "dance with me" rather than "dance on me." Although, they did mention that on occasion, a choreographer (at that time often a Russian) had an insight well beyond theirs, in which case they welcomed being "danced on."

Directors and showrunners almost always believe they have just such insight — it's only rarely true.

After three or four episodes of their show, the actors know their characters way better than a director who has come on just to direct episode five. A good set is ultimately controlled by the leading actors. Guest directors are just that, guests, and on occasions need to be reminded of that fact. The likelihood that they have a profound, novel insight to the world of your show is extremely unlikely, although they almost always claim they have such an insight. It's often how they got the directing job to begin with.

Another note about working with young directors: young directors are often considerable control freaks and don't like anyone on the set to know anything more about anything than they do. When working with such folks, it's often a good strategy to play dumb. Don't acknowledge that you know more about acting than they do. When asked how you like to work — and I truly apologize for this — say that you read the words and respond to them, period.

A WORD OF BIZ ADVICE

If the politics of the set are super toxic then just keep your head down and be sure to cash your check first thing.

METHODS FOR MAKING YOUR WORK MORE COMPELLING

Find the ordinary in the extraordinary and the extraordinary in the ordinary

As I mentioned before, this is a useful guide for character explorations — a goal hard to achieve, but worthy of the effort. For example, it's unlikely that Emily Dickinson went much of anywhere, but she created some of the most important poetry in the English language. Charlotte Brontë probably never met a man like Rochester in her life, but she dreamt him into existence. Artists who have never traveled must explore their world (an ordinary world) with a cruel intensity.

As well, people whose jobs move them into extraordinary circumstances often normalize them to be able to keep on keeping on. The first *Alien* film (before the arrival of the alien) is a classic example. The crew deal with their extraordinary interplanetary space travel as if it's no more than a UPS delivery service.

Remember to create people we would like to meet or people who thank the heavens we never have to meet. This basically applies to leads and high seconds (more on that later). But compelling does *not* mean eccentric.

What follows are some ways to make your work more compelling. Not every one of them applies to every actor, but once again, they are useful to have in your kitbag when you are not happy with the product you are creating.

The use of secrets: Hiding a dark secret inside an "ordinary" person can lead to great things. In Aaron Sorkin's *The West Wing*, Josh's secretary was only scheduled for an episode or two but ended up playing all six years of the series. Why? Because her secret yearning for Josh was compelling enough to keep her of interest to us, the viewer. In *Homicide: Life on the Street* (you can find full episodes on YouTube), Bayliss held the secret that he was raped by an uncle and it made his work more compelling to watch. It manifested in his ability to be civil with everyone except people he suspected of hurting children.

And another: Sam Waterson (as wonderfully talented as he is) floundered when he first took over *Law & Order* until he found a secret drinking problem. The role "landed" and he played with that as the hidden backstory for many years.

And one last one: the first season of *Homeland* was scheduled to have Damian Lewis's suspected terrorist character killed in two or three episodes. He played the entire season and parts of the next two as he brought the deepest, darkest secrets to set that explode in compelling moments. There are many more stories of actors who did *not* create secrets who ended up being dropped from shows, in some cases shows that had been written for them!

Force the State of Being to be in opposition to the Action: It produces a compelling juxtaposition and makes the moment more than the sum of its parts. So if the Action is to torture someone — surely a Left-Handed Action — then you have to make sure that you are sitting in a Right-Handed State of Being, such as I AM ASCENDING or I AM BEAUTIFUL or GOD IS IN HIS/HER/ITS HEAVEN AND ALL IS WELL IN THE WORLD, or the like. You will have to Key and Transfer the State of Being to make it work.

Fully investigate your knowledge of the metaphor of the Action: Bring your real knowledge to bear on the playing of that Action despite what the script might say. Actions are *not* plot points.

Fully investigate your knowledge of the Icon: Icons are the names of scenes, such as first kiss, first touch, first time, last time, the goodbye (see the list in chapter fifteen). Bring your full knowledge including any music, poetry or even dance that you associate with the Icon.

It is from the Icon and the metaphor of the Action that actors can draw upon their life knowledge independent of the script without doing harm to the script — it just gives it more depth and makes your work — big surprise: more compelling. But remember that your behavior is *not* who you are — and is not the part of yourself that the art of acting draws from.

Find and stay in Primary States of Being — and make them swing: For example, I SEE I LOVE, I KNOW I SHOULDN'T.

You can also develop swing by forcing a Right-Handed Primary against a Left-Handed Action and vice versa. This is elaborated elsewhere in the book.

Write better backstories: Actors who rely on writers to give them compelling backstories can wait a very long time. Actors must learn to think backwards. The text makes you do Y, so X must have happened before that made you then do Y. Stage actors look for that X in the scenes of the play; TV and film actors write whatever backstory they need to anchor Y. And unlike on the stage it doesn't have to have anything to do with the plot.

Use character modifiers: See following chapter.

Use action modifiers: See below.

A MOMENTARY ASIDE: THE IDEA OF THREE HEARTS

The Ancient Greeks believed we live in three hearts. The first is public — obvious. The second is private (for our significant other). The third, where our muse lives, and you only visit them after midnight, it's where your true self resides, safe from the staring eyes of the world.

It takes bravery to access your third heart — your muse is not always pleasant — but without possible pain there is no glory.

Do be aware that when you draw from that secret wellspring and the director or casting director (or your significant other, for that matter) doesn't like your performance — well, they don't like what is quint-essentially you. It's the real you that is on display, not your acting. It's so hard to get Present and get down to your real self that it is deflating when the director's response to your hard work is something like, "Can you do that facing a little more to the left?" Sure, do it a little more to the left, but still access your hidden self. Nonetheless, if you don't access your real self, it's hard for the work to rise above the mediocre.

ANOTHER ASIDE: THE WILLINGNESS TO BE BORING

Actors also need bravery to be boring. Stage actors resist this like crazy, but it often throws performances over the top, which is the ultimate in boring. In this case allowing yourself to be boring means that you don't have to *be doing things*. High seconds do things — George does things. Jerry thinks — Jerry's the lead — and he chances being boring by not doing things, but by thinking about doing things. (If you don't know these characters go to YouTube and watch an episode or two or twenty of *Seinfeld*.)

MODIFIERS OF ACTION

There are ways of making the playing of your Actions more compelling — they are called modifiers, in that they modify the Action, not change it — just as an adjective describes a noun but doesn't change it. The word "blue" modifies the noun "chair" in the phrase "I sat in the blue chair." Blue doesn't change the reality that you are sitting in a chair, it elaborates what kind of chair.

Drivers, as discussed previously, determine the intensity of the playing of Action — answering the question: How much? Make the Driver more imminent and the Action will be pushed forward, sometimes to the point of violence.

But there are other modifiers of Action that are not Drivers but actor choices that enable the actor to bring more interest to the work.

1. Relationship

TV and film acting requires actors to define a reality within families. The reason for this is very simple: your TV show has to be shown in Jonestown, Ohio, and Johannesburg, South Africa, and the only constant is family. So, we are talking about all family members and then lover/lover in opposition to husband/wife.

When I teach, I usually sit in older brother — or, if they force me, father, which I often resist. Despite the fact that teaching in LA is completely different than teaching in Toronto or Vancouver or over Zoom — the thing that is constant is my familial relationship to the actors. Some actors play mother to me (which I do not resist but I inform them that that is what they are doing), father to me (very rare) or older brother/sister. And yes, the danger zone lover/lover comes up sometimes. All of these modulations are done in order to get my points across to the actors — as a teacher you play Actions too!

If you want to watch a genius at shifting relationships — watch Jimmy Stewart's work — especially in *Harvey*. He starts a scene with the young nurse in older brother then drops into younger brother, then plays a beat in husband/wife, then one in lover/lover, then plays a moment near the end of the scene in younger sister.

Although breaking things into genders is an antiquated way of thinking — it remains a useful tool in both analyzing problems in scenes and offering actors a new tack on a scene.

2. Room in a House

This is one of the few techniques in this book that you cannot use on the stage. In TV or film if the setting is a bedroom there is a bed and a desk and a pennant and the other paraphernalia we usually associate with a bedroom. The visual tells us where we are.

On the stage, in a play like Brecht's *Baal* that takes place in dozens of different locales the set might be nothing more than a raked floor with a red splotch on a backdrop. An actor turns over a chair and all the actors have to play as if the chair is a kitchen stove. Not in TV and film. Because the visual looks after the geography the actor is free to play the scene as if it is in another room in a house in order to make the playing of the Action more interesting.

So here's the paradigm: if you understand the metaphor of the Action in your <u>head</u> but not your <u>heart</u>, you use the room in the house that you feel most powerful in. But — if you really get the metaphor of the Action in your heart then you choose the room in the house you feel weakest in — all in an effort to make your acting more compelling.

So here are the basic rooms in a house that actors use. (Each has to be Keyed and Transferred to make it work!)

- The bedroom that you think of as the room in which you grew up
- A sibling's bedroom
- A parent or parents' bedroom
- The kitchen
- A parent's office if they had one in the house
- A dining room/eating area (if the family sat down on occasions to eat together)
- A lover's bedroom
- A dream room
- This one only works in cold climates: the furnace room, where the brave kid hid behind the furnace when you played hide-and-seek, where your brother brought home a garter snake three years ago and it got out of its cage and every six months you find a shedded skin down there, a room of horror and bravery

Note that the living room is not included — it's neutral.

3. Time of Day

Again, in TV and film, the visual will look after this but if, for example, you feel very strong in the morning, then use that when the Action is in your head not your heart.

If you are really weak in the morning then use that when the Action is solidly ensconced in your heart.

If you examine the day carefully there are strong and weak parts. They vary with individuals but, do spot the times when you are strongest and weakest — it becomes part of your knowledge base from which to work.

4. Time of Year

Well, this doesn't work so well in Los Angeles, but in Toronto February is definitely not August. Again, pick out which months make you feel strongest and which weakest and apply them appropriately.

A FEW CAVEATS

- In moments of peak performance — when everything in the text rings infinitely true to you — do not use any modifiers.
- Both the young and the old are compelling by the fact that they are so different from the majority of us. As are the very tall, the very beautiful, the very heavy, etc.
- Compelling must *not* be eccentric! TV and film are broadcast media and must on some level hit the center of the audience's thinking.
- If any of this gets in the way of communicating clearly — i.e., sending simple, honest signals, then don't use it. At the base level an actor is a communications artist.
- If any of this throws you off of who you are,

don't use it. Never jettison the real self, your Ethos!

- Sorry, but none of these are tricks. All of them take time and patience and diligence to make them work for you.

MORE TOOLS TO MAKE THE WORK MORE COMPELLING

Cri de coeur: a line (or word sequence) of text that *you* speak that delineates character and often specifies class. It's worth searching out and often is more apparent in high seconds than in firsts (leads). In high seconds it points toward the predicated behavior of the character. In firsts, it often points towards the class structure. It's another useful tool.

"Women and children can be careless, but not men" is a classic cri de coeur that Brando says to Michael in *The Godfather*.

Here's another one from Mark Twain: "But I do have certain rules that I make sure that I follow: I never smoke more than one cigar at a time — I have no other restrictions."

Stumbles/obstacles: come from the old method language but can be useful tools. There are interior stumbles/obstacles which are actually swings. I want X but why the fuck do I want X or there can be a repercussion if I try to get X. Then there are exterior stumbles/obstacles that are presented by your acting partner or sometimes by circumstance. It's ultimately a more useful idea in the theater, where you can stabilize scenes, as opposed to in TV and film, where stability is the enemy of immediacy.

Charismatic points: at times you will find sections of text that are so profoundly honest to you that you need do nothing more than breathe down and say the truth. My daughter was a nationally ranked hockey player, and from an early age she played a ton of games. I do remember one day where I watched her play three games in a tournament and her team lost all three by a single goal — two in overtime. That night she came into our bedroom and sat on the edge of the bed. "You okay, Beth?" She turned to me and said simply — honesty, profoundly: "We lost a lot of games." She was sitting in a charismatic point and simply spoke the truth — it made me both laugh and cry at the same time.

The carving of interior landscapes: I have a strong memory of a famous actor in the '80s being interviewed by a novice from a local Toronto newspaper. She kept pressing him to talk about character, which he resisted until finally he said something like, "I carve interior landscapes — hills and valleys and cliffs and rivers and mountains — then I pull out my back ribs and allow the air to glide over the interior landscape I have produced. The air — my breath — picks up the characteristics of the hills and valleys and rivers and mountains so that when it leaves my mouth it carries those flavors. That's what acting is." I've tried to find the exact quote but have been unable to do so, so it's possible that this is a false memory — although it being false does not mean it is not true.

The crevice: you can change the canvas upon which you paint by creating interior crevices in your character. It's a complicated and sometimes excruciatingly slow process — not something that you can leap at — which is the tendency of most actors. We're looking for hidden things (crevices), secrets you think you couldn't possibly share with anyone — often to do with sex, racism, violence, dreams of conquest, antisocial things. Then you need to open them up — allow them into your heart and live with them for a while.

Some universities are terrified to approach these ideas. But it's a potent tool if you just sit with the thoughts and allow the thoughts to infiltrate your very self. And those thoughts will lead you to secrets.

Secrets are the crevices of character. When you find them, don't share them, nurture them — often in the dark. Back to the Greek notion of a third heart where your muse lives.

Often the most interesting thing about a character is the crevice — the hidden hollow that makes them different from the rest of us but *not* eccentric.

In a casting room about 80 percent of the actors can "do" the audition scene. The object is for you to stand out in the audition room *without* being actory. One of the ways to do that is with the use of crevices.

TO SUM UP:

1. Be compelling, not necessarily right.
2. Beware of ensemble or "family" politics on set.
3. Your real audience is a producer far away who could want you for their next project.
4. Make a director work through you not on top of you.
5. Be wary of young directors who have only one idea how a scene must be done.
6. Guest directors don't know more about your show than you do.
7. Find the ordinary in the extraordinary and extraordinary in the ordinary.
8. Create people we would like to meet or people we are grateful we will never meet.

   - Use secrets.
   - Write better backstories to be more compelling.
   - Force the Action in opposition to the State of Being.
   - Investigate what you know about the Icon and the metaphor of the Action.
   - Find and stay in Primary States of Being and make them swing.
   - Action modifiers: relationship within family, room in a house, time of year, time of day.

- Further tools to use: cri de coeur, stumbles/obstacles, charismatic points, carving of interior landscapes and the crevice.

CHAPTER 9

Tool #2 — Drone Noting

In any numbered scene in a film or TV script, there is a moment of most intense pleasure or pain that your character actually says — or should say.

It's the Drone Note. (For those of you who are Meisner actors it's best to do the repetition exercise on the Drone Note.)

Drone Noting works this way: your significant other has been coming home later and later and finally you wait up for them and at four o'clock in the morning you hear your apartment door open. What you want to say to them is "*WHERE THE FUCK HAVE YOU BEEN?*" (the Drone), but if your writer has any talent they won't make you say that, they'll make you state a fact — in this case: "*IT'S LATE.*"

The line *IT'S LATE* works because it sits over top of the Drone *WHERE THE FUCK HAVE YOU BEEN?* The tension between that which you *want* to say and that which you *choose* to say makes the moment work. The actor's prep is on the Drone Note, *not* the spoken line.

Another example. In Pinter's brilliant play *Betrayal*, when the husband finds out that his wife has been having an affair with his best friend, Jerry, he says, "You know I've always rather liked Jerry. I've liked him rather more than I've liked you. I should have had an affair with him myself."

This bizarre statement sits over top of the unspoken Drone of "How could you?" Once again, the actor work is on the Drone Note, not the line.

In *The Godfather*, Michael approaches his father in the garden. As he nears, something very dark crosses Brando's face (it's the Drone Note) and Michael sees it and says something like (this section of text is paraphrased so that I can illustrate a point. The actual dialogue is below): "What's wrong, Dad?" Brando raises his glass of wine and says, "I drink too much." Michael responds, "You're an old man, you're allowed to drink." Then Brando asks, "Have you had the phones tapped?" Michael responds, "Of course, Dad. What?" Brando ignores the question and asks his own. "And you know the one who calls will be the traitor?" To which Michael responds, "Yes, I know, Dad. What?" Then Brando gets up and moves from frame left to frame right (for no particular reason) and when he sits, he says the Drone Note: "I never wanted this for you, Michael — for Sonny, yes, but never for you."

That Drone Note was percolating in Brando from the top of the scene. It's what makes his opening line, about drinking too much, work — that which he wants to say roils under a statement of fact.

For those of you with directing ambitions, when Brando sits frame right as he says the Drone Note, the Drone Note of the music in the soundtrack comes up.

Here's the actual dialogue. Note the repetition of the phrase "What's the matter, what's bothering you?" It implies that Michael senses the Drone Note beneath Brando's lines.

> BRANDO
> Barzini will move against you
> first. He'll set up a meeting
> with someone you absolutely
> trust. Guaranteeing your
> safety. And at that meeting
> you'll be assassinated. I like
> to drink wine more than I used
> to. Anyway, I'm drinking more.

> MICHAEL
> It's good for you, Pop.

> BRANDO
> I don't know. Are you happy
> with your wife and children?

> MICHAEL
> Very happy.

> BRANDO
> That's good. I hope you don't
> mind the way I keep going over
> this Barzini business.

> MICHAEL
> No, not at all.

> BRANDO
> It's an old habit. I spend my
> life trying not to be careless.

Women and children can be
careless, but not men. How's
your boy?

MICHAEL
He's good. He looks more like
you every day. He's smarter
than I am. He's three and can
read the funny papers.

BRANDO
Read the funny papers. I want
you to arrange for a telephone
man to check all in- and
outgoing calls.

MICHAEL
I did it already. I took care
of that, Pop.

BRANDO
That's right. I forgot.

MICHAEL
What's the matter? What's
bothering you? I'll handle it.
I told you I can handle it, so
I'll handle it.

BRANDO
I knew that Santino would have
to go through all this. And
Fredo . . . Fredo was, well
. . . But I never wanted this
for you.

The side trips to talk about Michael's son are a way of delaying the saying of the Drone Note, but even those lines have the Drone Note boiling beneath them.

Drone Noting is a particularly good technique for stage-trained actors. One of the many complaints about stage-trained actors on TV or film sets (and there are many) is that they take too damned long to emotionally "get in."

There's very little preamble in TV or film scripts, and even if there is, no one — not even the Czechs (although I've been informed that sometimes they still do) — shoots in sequence, so an actor has to be able to jump in feetfirst emotionally and land those Primary States of Being without a "glide path" to the emotion.

The playwright Edward Bond makes the same request of his actors in his preamble to the updated *Narrow Road to the Deep North*. He requests that actors become emotional gymnasts.

Drone Noting allows an actor to cut to the chase, to start with the first blood — pick your favorite cliché — but it's important to be able to do. No one has time or interest on set in helping an actor get to the required emotional level. It's actor work, and, unlike in a stage rehearsal, there's no dramaturg or kindly assistant director to ease you in. On set it's more likely that they'll yell at you to "fucking get going, we're losing the light!"

Also, there are no eight-hour rehearsal days. If there is any rehearsal (and there isn't always), it is brief and as much to assure the director that they have their cameras in the right positions as it is to explore the scene on an acting level.

Although it may be an apocryphal story, I'm going to repeat it because it's instructive. So, the story goes that Ingmar Bergman, the famous Swedish film director, was asked to direct a production of Ibsen's *Hedda Gabler* at the National Theatre in London. And, as the story goes, he wanted to cut the entire first act of the play and replace it with a beautiful woman in a diaphanous nightgown running down a curved staircase at the bottom of which she vomits and says, "Oh God." Blackout. End of act one.

Bergman's act one tells the audience everything they learn in the normal forty minutes of Ibsen's first act: beautiful woman, pregnant, doesn't want to be.

As I said, I have no idea if this is true — I never saw the production and don't know anyone who did — and I assume that the National Theatre rejected the idea, but the idea is good, and on the directorial level close to what an actor does when they Drone Note to get in at the top of a scene.

As a sidebar it's interesting that Brando so often used Drone Noting since it is at least partially a non-method way of working, and he was considered to be the great method actor of his time.

TO SUM UP:

1. Drone Notes are moments of most intense pain or pleasure that you say or ought to say.

2. Actors work on the Drone Notes (open them up) to make statements of fact work.
3. Once you say your Drone Note you can jump to another one.
4. Watching Brando's use of Drone Notes is an education in how the art of acting works.

CHAPTER 10

Some Notes on Character

FIRSTS (LEADS) VS HIGH SECONDS VS THIRDS

There are three categories of roles: firsts, high seconds and thirds. Each category of character is created differently. Firsts get to tinker with only four variables in the creation of character. They are:

1. country vs city
2. age up or down (playing at the oldest you can or the youngest you can)
3. class up or down (often the most crucial of the four)
4. married vs single (where married only really pertains to children, not spouse)

The choices are often dictated by your character's job. For example, a doctor is usually city, age up, upper-middle class, married. A social worker is city, age up, lower-middle class (like cops and firemen), married.

In *Seinfeld*, Jerry is the first and he is city, single (although married to his lifestyle)/age down, upper-middle class.

In *Hamlet*, Prince Hamlet is city, age up, married (if he isn't married to Denmark much of the play makes no sense), upper class.

Despite the demands of the role, most firsts *play* married in that they have a concern above and beyond their own gratification. The old theater term for this was "it gives a character feet." Children become an obvious source of such grounding although even actors with children often have trouble Keying and Transferring their kids into their work. What most actors use is the possibility of a sick parent.

It works this way: Say you are offered a six-month contract in Alaska with the only downside being that you will be out of cell phone (or even SAT) range for the better part of the time. If you do not have children and if your parents are well then take the job — go to Alaska before it becomes nothing more than an oil field. But if your mom is sick, then your decision of going or not going to Alaska and being out of contact for six months is way more compelling to watch. Remember, the object is to be compelling!

Another example. Two young people are sitting side by side in a bar. They begin to do the "are we going to go home together or not" dance. If both are single then either do it or don't do it, but be safe. However, if one (or both) of you has a little boy at home who cries every time you leave the house, then your decision swings between your desire on one hand and your obligation to the boy on the other — and hence is more compelling for us to watch.

Before the question is asked — here's the answer. No, it doesn't matter if the entire story is about being single and trying to get married. Take a look at the old TV show *Ally McBeal*. The entire show is about her trying to find a marriageable partner — yet she, as a lead, plays married. Playing a person with a married person's obligation makes performance deeper.

Jerry and Hamlet are firsts. George and the Player King are high seconds. When playing high seconds, you have the same four choices to make, but you also have predicated behavior that you have to incorporate.

So, George is city, age down, upper-middle class, single *and* he must be willing to climb tall blond women and fall on his silly head, then get back up and find another.

The Player King is country, age up, working class, married *and* he must be bombastic.

The thirds are Kramer and the Grave Digger. In both of these cases *behavior* dominates to the point that we don't know much about their background. Kramer is just this thing that explodes into rooms while the Grave Digger is little more than a profound cynic. It's not surprising that thirds are often cast from the ranks of comedians.

With firsts we do stories about you and your work, you and your coworkers and you and your love life. With high seconds we usually do stories about two of those three. With thirds, we are just interested in behavior.

Firsts almost always swing — either on the Action (I want X but why do I want X) or from the Action to the State of Being (one on the left and one on the right). Firsts are almost always liberals because liberals swing. Even as a person is approaching a liberal with a drawn knife, it occurs to a liberal that the poor thing probably had a tough childhood — or the like.

Firsts always see "the line in the sand." Jerry wants to know if they're real. But he knows that if he asks, it's possible that he may lose this girl — the line in the sand. George (the second) doesn't even realize that there is a line in the sand and simply asks, "Hey, are those real?" If Elaine hadn't beaten him to it, Kramer (the third) would have tripped and fallen and grabbed, then announced "Hey, they're real." (Once again, you can go to YouTube and find this reference — or ask a friend, if you do not know it.)

Once you've settled on your choices about country vs city, age up vs age down, class up vs class down, married vs single — and the director has agreed but is still not completely satisfied (usually expressed by the director with such insightful phrases as "a little more oomph," "you know what I mean," "it's close but not there yet," "just doesn't get me," etc.) then you go to modifiers.

Back to being compelling:

CHARACTER MODIFIERS

What Music is inside your character? Characters, just like people, have a soundtrack to their lives. For years we knew when our next-door neighbor's little boy was approaching because, like many young boys, he sang his soundtrack out loud — in his case Darth Vader's theme music. Change the music inside the character and you change the character without altering the basics of class, age, marriage, etc. A Hamlet who has a 50 Cent tune inside him is profoundly different than a Hamlet who has a Baroque quartet inside him.

What does your character call private parts? A Hamlet who refers to it as his manhood is quite different than a Hamlet who calls it his pee-pee.

What does your character think will happen to them after they die? When I first arrived in New York City I remember walking by the UN building and seeing the statue of Dag Hammarskjöld (an early and brilliant secretary-general of the UN). It was the cutline beneath the statue that drew my attention: "You can't understand how a man lives his life until you understand what he thinks is going to happen to him after he dies."

I remember chortling as I read it. Religion was on the retreat back then to the point that many of us believed it would disappear altogether. Even a cursory look at the world today tells you that we were wrong.

If your character believes that there is judgment after death, then it completely influences the way that they live. If your character believes that you die and then return in another form (wolverine or two-humped camel are my personal favorites), that too has behavior ramifications.

Then there is a third option, which I first heard brilliantly expressed in a restaurant in New York, where, as in so many eating establishments there, a couple was talking way too loudly. Over my omelet I heard a fifty-ish woman exclaim very loudly, "What?" To which her fifty-ish husband responded, "As I said, no, we have no life insurance. None." To which she demanded, "Why?" and he responded, "Cause when I die the world ends."

That's a third position your character may have vis-à-vis their passing.

There's also a fourth position, the *Fame* position. If you were subjected to this TV show you may remember its opening shot of young people, vaulting over parked cars and singing in an alley. The lyrics they were singing included this phrase "we are going to live forever." Well, that's the fourth position.

Is your character a three-legged dog? When a dog loses a leg, it does not look backward — it manages as best it can to walk on three legs and carries on. Is your character like that, or do they carry the baggage of past failures? Two very different kinds of characters.

Does your character pull the goalie? This one comes from Malcolm Gladwell's podcast *Revisionist History*. Mathematically, if your hockey team (Go Leafs Go! Am I the only one who finds it odd that the plural for Leaf is NOT Leaves but rather Leafs — although "Go Leaves Go" does seem like a spring-cleaning motto) is behind by one goal in the third period, math dictates that your best chance of winning the game is to pull your goalie with between four and six minutes left in the game. If you are behind by two goals, you should pull the goalie with about ten minutes left. If you are behind by three or more goals, you should begin the third period with no goalie in your net.

No one does this because it's much more likely that the team with their goalie still in the net will score than the team that chose to use an extra attacker by removing their goalie.

But it doesn't make sense. It is no better to lose 3–2 than to lose 12–2. Losing is losing. And leaving your goalie in pretty much guarantees that you will lose.

People don't pull the goalie for fear that they will look stupid. 12–2 sure does look stupider than 3–2 *but* a loss is a loss.

Does your character pull the goalie, i.e., does the character care what others think about them? There is a lot of freedom in not caring what others think, but it's a lonely place to be. Check out the characters in *The Big Short* — some pull the goalie, some do not.

What does the character dream about? What awakens them laughing? What awakens them screaming? Change the dreams and you will have changed the character.

TO SUM UP:

1. Characters are divided into firsts, high seconds and thirds.

2. Firsts get to choose between country vs city, age up/down, class up/down, married vs single.

3. High seconds have the same four choices *plus* a predicated behavior.

4. Thirds are all behavior and often cast from the ranks of comedians.

5. Firsts swing, almost always play married, always see the "line in the sand."

6. Character modifiers:

   - What music is inside them?
   - What do they call private parts?
   - What do they think will happen to them after they die?
   - Do they carry baggage from the past or move on?
   - Do they care what others think of them?
   - What do they dream about?

CHAPTER 11

Principle #3 —
Modern Acting Is About Selecting Not Pretending

"All good things come by grace . . . and grace
comes by art, and art does not come easy."
— NORMAN MACLEAN, *A RIVER RUNS THROUGH IT*

With rare exceptions modern acting is about selecting
not pretending. Although we have some famous trans-
formation actors, the majority of professional actors
make their living by selecting from parts of themselves
rather than pasting things onto their exterior. But if
working from "outside in" works for you, so be it. You can
skip this chapter.

Actors need a wide array of "self" to select from. It's
why an actor needs to understand that a concert violinist
is willing to pay a half a million dollars for an instrument.
Surely his or her technique is just as good on a $300
violin as it is on a $500,000 violin. But the violinist can't
make "most eloquent music" on the cheaper instrument
and hence is willing to pay for the finer one.

An actor's instrument (that which they get to select
from) is themselves. And this instrument must be worked

on to make sure that it is as complex and deep and profound as possible — a $500,000 instrument if you will.

How does one work on their instrument? Many ways. Voice and movement class are sometimes the entry ways to personal growth. Breath in the body is often a revelation. Making sure that your knees are directly over your feet also can change some things in an actor. But it's not just classes that expand an actor's instrument. That instrument is expanded by life experience and by consciously seeking out "voyages."

VOYAGING

There's every reason to believe that the very first actor was some brave soul who voyaged into the dangerous valley, found something of value then returned and standing by the nighttime fire told the rest (who had not voyaged) of what they had found. It was the fact of the voyage *and* the return with something of value that gave the person the right to speak.

Literally to stand in the light — as an actor does.

Modern actors have to earn the right to speak, as well as to have their faces three times the size of god when on a movie screen. To do so they have to voyage and come back with something of value.

Actors must figure out a way to voyage and return, literally sometimes, but often metaphorically. Sometimes in dreams. Some actors find Malcolm Godwin's book *The Lucid Dreamer* both interesting and helpful.

To be able to speak with authority — enough authority so the audience will "lend me your ears" — one must have traveled into the valley, up the mountain, into the sea, then returned to tell us what they found.

I can't tell you the number of productions of *A Midsummer Night's Dream* that I've seen and been annoyed by Titania's speech at the beginning of the third act where she tells us about her night of joyful sex with Bottom (who was then a donkey). I don't need the actress to be a sexual all-star, but she has to know at least a few things about sex that we in the audience don't know.

I directed a production of *Don Juan in Hell* with an extremely talented actor playing the lead. Six days before we were to open, he told me that he needed two days off. I'm not sure what he did in those two days, but upon his return his Don Juan made much more sense than before he left.

I'm not asking actors to endanger themselves in order to find compelling truths in themselves, but they have to at least work at it — and research it.

For those of us who have had a parent go through the hideousness of Alzheimer's disease it's offensive to watch an actor schmact their way through the mad scenes in *King Lear*. It's not hard to at least observe those who are afflicted with this awful disease that you are supposedly portraying!

Schmact is an appropriate term — it is the coarse act of pretending to know something or feel something when in fact you don't know or feel anything! It's just pretend!

A word of warning: you cannot voyage through watching theater, film or television. These are completed products — they cannot be dreamt upon. Once you've seen Brando do Stanley in *Streetcar*, that's Stanley in *Streetcar*. When the old Disney cartoon *Fantasia*, an animated version à la MTV but of classical music that came out in June of 1941 (told you it was old), some discerning critics realized the limitations these visuals put on the music. Dancing hippos have nothing to do with the classical piece they illustrate, but every time you hear that music your mind jumps to those dancing hippos. *Fantasia* limits our ability to dream on the music, which is one of the great gifts of music — especially music without lyrics.

Solidified images such as TV, film and theater do not allow you to freely voyage, they control where the voyage goes.

Some of the older European theater schools have their actors read novels (yes, as a novelist myself I acknowledge my prejudice) rather than plays. The novelist tells you how the character thinks. The playwright tells you what they say. More importantly, there is no visual to control your dreaming in a novel.

If you look at Victorian novels sometimes there are ten pages of what he is thinking, then you get to his dialogue: "Yes." Then ten more pages of thought and his line: "No." The thoughts, not the dialogue, are crucial to leading actors. We pay leading actors for what they *think*, not what they *do*.

TO SUM UP:

1. Modern acting is basically about selecting not pretending.
2. Voyaging: literal or metaphoric is an important part of an actor's arsenal.
3. You cannot voyage through television, film or theater.

CHAPTER 12

A Tangent — The Voice in Your Head

I grant that this is off on a tangent, but it's important to address the voice in your head that reads the lines to you as your eyes scan the script. That voice gives you intonation, line readings and even blocking, but it's on the whole class-A bullshit.

Twenty years ago, I would have told actors that that voice was their first impression and that they should follow it. Now I tell actors that if they have a teacher who claims that the voice in your head is your first impression, they should seriously consider getting another acting teacher.

That voice is not *your* voice, it's the voice of media.

It you were sentient for the past thirty years you have been inundated with media. Movies, TV, Spotify, YouTube, podcasts, audiobooks, endless advertising, etc. The average American apparently watches four hours of television a day — wow! And this was true before streaming — can you imagine watching four hours of broadcast television daily?

Media is so pervasive that just watching people on the street you will see that they are imitating what they saw on TV. For example, cops wouldn't know how to get out of their cars and approach a stopped vehicle if they hadn't seen it done dozens of times on TV. But this is backwards — art is supposed to imitate life *not* vice versa. And often the art they are imitating is truly questionable. So now young actors looking to emulate behavior and watching those around them may in fact not be seeing real behavior but imitation of bad "art." Once again: art is supposed to imitate life — not vice versa. This is distressing to say the least.

Years ago, I was sitting in a restaurant in New York with a group of actors and a very famous director came rushing in. He was very upset. There had been a terrible subway accident and people had been badly hurt. He had been on one of the trains — but above and beyond the injuries — what really upset him was, and I really can't forget his statement, "The survivors weren't seeing what was really right there in front of them — they were responding the way TV told them to fucking respond. It was sickening."

So, here's the acting problem this creates, and that every actor who has done a lot of shooting knows. The writer probably wrote the script with the voice of media in his or her head. The director's first response to the work has the voice of media in their head, which leads them to set up their cameras to capture the voice of media. If you agree to perform that voice of media/voice in your head (which everyone in the audition room can do — see chapter seventeen) then you will agree to be mediocre. And most directors won't fight that. Mediocrity allows them to shine — be careful.

When do you use the voice in your head? The same situations that you would use beat play — when working opposite amateurs, kids or animals. Or, let's be business honest, on Friday afternoons on series TV.

HOW DO I GET AROUND THE VOICE IN MY HEAD?

1. Find the metaphor of the Action and go back to your own life to open the truth/s in that. Key and Transfer when necessary — find the poetry, painting, dance, etc., of it and commit to winning your Action.
2. Find the Icon, apply it to your own life and bring real things to the material.
3. Double clutch, as in baseball: don't follow your first choice. You may think it's a fastball, but you have to wait to see the spin to know for sure.
4. Make a director direct through you (dance *with* you) not on top of you (dance *on* you).

Do remember that if you are reduced to playing the voice in your head, you have been reduced to being mediocre and since an actor's prime directive is be compelling, this is clearly wrong. A caveat: there are times, after real exploration, you will come back to the voice in your head and see that it actually is your real response to the material. If so, then use it. But only after trying everything else!

ABOUT WORKING WITH DIRECTORS

Allow yourself to gather as much information on the director as you can. Be aware that what you have collected is just folks' opinions and that your experience with the director may be much better than theirs. Be sure to see their last film or TV show. On set, be as open with the director as you can — try to really find them the way you would find an acting partner. Always be aware when they are falling behind and therefore getting a lot of pressure to get back on schedule. Pick your fights: don't fight about everything, but if choices are being made that throw you off your center (pull you away from your ethos), if a costume simply makes no sense with the class (upper/lower/middle) you are playing, if a director's choice is antithetic to what you have already shot, or if they insist on shooting in Secondary States of Being so that they can get endless pretty pictures — then you may have to do battle.

Do be aware that directors doing their first major production are under tremendous pressure to prove that they deserve to direct — so cut them a break for the first little while. Once they get those first few days in the can, on time and approved by the upper echelons, then you can begin to gently challenge them on their choices. Until then they can't get known as an "actor's director" (from the crew's point of view, an awful thing), because they have to demonstrate to everyone that they are capable, in control and can guide this huge enterprise safely to harbor. So, as much as they might see your point and want to give you what you want, they may have to resist at first.

TO SUM UP:

1. The voice in your head is the voice of media, not your real response to the script.
2. To get around the voice in your head return to Icons and Action metaphors.
3. Pick your fights on the basis of what is *really* important to you and your character.

CHAPTER 13

Principle #4 —
No Neutral Mask

Out of the PC frying pan into the PC fire — politically correct folks sharpen your knives, start your engines, or whatever revving-up cliché you like.

A neutral mask implies that any actor can play any role. But when even stage audition notices sound like TV audition notices (specifying sex, job, age, marriage status, etc.), the very idea (good or bad) of a neutral mask in professional acting is a rarity. This is especially true in broadcast media, and only a little less true in film and streaming.

Your appearance will, at least initially, dominate your casting. It is the canvas upon which you paint. I call it your Hit.

You are not necessarily your Hit, but you'll learn a lot about your Hit simply by the way that the world treats you.

We read Hits all the time. If you ever were a server in a restaurant (and what actor hasn't done this kind of work?) then you know exactly what I'm talking about. You take one look at a table and you know that they will be there the whole damned night, share one pitcher of cheap draft beer and leave you a sodden dollar bill under a half-empty glass. And you're seldom wrong. If you are wrong too often as a server, you will never make the tips necessary to survive.

Women read men's Hits every time they walk into an elevator and the door begins to close. They have to be safe. At the end of classes at my studio in Toronto — often close to midnight — I don't even look as I make my way to my car, but I make sure that the women are escorted to safe subway stops.

When I returned to Toronto after all those years in New York it freaked me out that you couldn't walk through the subway cars (this was before the open cars on the north-south line). In New York — especially if you were going to the South Bronx to watch the Yankees — you looked at your fellow passengers and quickly decided whether it was safe or not. And how did you do this? You read Hits. And if it wasn't safe or comfortable you moved to the next car.

I openly grant there are troubling aspects of this.

If you want to test your class status in Toronto doll yourself up, then go to one of the high-end stores at Hazelton Lanes. Many of the salespeople who work there make most of their money on commission. They take one look at you and know whether you can afford a $1,169.99 sweater (before HST) or not. And if not, they won't spend time with you. How do they know? They read your Hit.

And no — it's not just clothing. When you go to the courthouses to watch trials (something I suggest actors should do), you will never mistake a secretary for a lawyer. They may both wear silk blouses, but the lawyer carries herself in a different way than the secretary and, by the by, probably comes from a different class.

Your Hit consists of only four things: country vs city; married vs single (which only has to do with children not spouse); age up vs age down and class up vs class down, as we saw in chapter ten.

In my studio I always allow the new actors to read my Hit first. It does a few important things. It gives them permission to really see and give expression to what they see. It also establishes that honesty is important in the studio and their art, and that honesty requires bravery.

We start with country vs city and they all correctly label me city. Then I ask them why and promise *not* to be offended. They usually start with the way I speak, but I cut them off and startle them when I say, "'Cause Jews don't live in the country."

This despite the fact that my family could very well have been many generations deep in Canada and for a long time lived on a small farm north of Coburg, Ontario. It *doesn't matter*. People who look like me (and no you really can't overcome your look, because it is the canvas upon which you are going to apply pigment) live in cities.

Then I ask them my class structure and they easily guess upper-middle class — clearly educated, etc. At this point I mention that many people who look like me (Polish/Russian Ashkenazi Jews) live extremely modest lives (I even name the districts in Toronto where they live), but the predominant response to my Hit is upper-middle class.

Then I ask them what the bottom of my playing age is and they usually are way too gracious — it's about sixty. Then I ask for the top — they usually go silent. It's sixty-eight. Then I show them how to modulate between my bottom and my top. "When I think of myself as Dr. Cyril Rotenberg's son, I'm at my youngest. When I think of myself as Joey and Beth's dad, I'm my oldest." This only works if you are connected to the deep sense of yourself and are Present. If you are, all you need to do is drop a stone (an Image) into the deep well of the self and it will cause ripples in the pool. Ripples up in age or down in age — nothing to do with limping, gray hair or the like.

Finally, I ask them if I am married or single and they all chime in married, and indeed I am, because I carry my kids with me in my Hit and would even if I was divorced.

For myself — if the audition criteria are male, fifty-five to sixty-five, doctor, married — my only question: is do you want me to wear my brown suit or my blue one? My Hit alone satisfies the character criteria, so no modulation is required.

Once again, you are not necessarily your Hit, but you *must* learn to be able to play your Hit to get into this business. It is your way in!

Yes, there are modulators for your Hit. One, strangely, is symmetry: if you bring both of your parents equally into your Hit, then we will have a tendency to say country. If you part your hair equally, once again we will have a tendency to identify you as country.

Class structure is actually most important when it comes to casting. Over and over again talented actors uncast themselves because they present in the wrong class. Class structure has to do with horizon and expectation. Simplistically: a working-class kid wants a car; a middle-class kid wants a good car; an upper-class kid wants several very good cars.

It's instructive to watch high school parent-teacher meetings. Huge numbers of Ontario students aren't able to pass the newly rigorous math requirement in the province. When working-class parents hear this, some of them respond that they were never very good in math and they make a fine living without it. When a middle-class parent is told that little Tommy is failing math, most blame the teacher and hire tutors. Upper-class parents usually don't hear the same thing because they have kids in private schools where sometimes the fix is in.

Which leads me to the anomalies of class structure in North America because it's not always based on income. For example, every unionized worker at the Ford plant makes more money than almost everyone who works in publishing, but the workers at the Ford plant are working class and the workers in publishing are middle class.

Another way of looking at class structure: you are throwing a house party and your significant other informs you that there are three men in the kitchen who no one knows, and they are drinking all the beer. This is not a problem for working-class men. They bring the women to the front of the house and take care of the matter. It's not a problem for upper-class people because they actually hire professional security — the problem is for middle-class people — who have the awful tendency of trying to make friends with people who hate them.

To be blunt: if the role requires a sixty-year-old Puerto Rican woman with a hair lip — I'm sure there are three such underused, extremely talented SAG actors waiting in Los Angeles.

I grant that big stars are now getting involved in playing outside their Hits — Russell Crowe is brilliant as Roger Ailes in *The Loudest Voice*, and you can name some others.

But when you start out, you play what you look like. You inhabit your Hit so that you actually present the auditioner with "someone who looks like me would play this role this way."

We had a rather famous incident like this years ago in Toronto when they were looking to cast a fiftyish Polish detective. A powerful agent got her young, handsome actor into the room. He made no attempt to be either fifty or Polish but showed them how someone with his Hit would play the role. He got cast (which then required the writer to rewrite much of the script, illustrating the hierarchy of power in TV).

So, here are some caveats about Hit reading. Anyone who knows/loves you can't read your Hit. They see well past your appearance. It's why you should never show your 8x10s to your family. They will always pick the wrong picture. People new to North America cannot accurately read your Hit. They will read your Hit based upon the movies they've seen from this part of the world — not a reliable source.

On occasion an actor is so profoundly different from their Hit that something has to be done. I taught an actor who is now quite popular, who asked to have a cup of coffee after our first class. I agreed and saw that she was very upset by the Hit I'd pinned on her — city/age down/class way up/single.

She told me only a bit of her personal history, and she was anything but the Hit I had read. I told her to clear some time in her schedule. After each class, I toured her through a wealthy part of town and said, "You were raised in that house, your boyfriend in this one. You went to this school. You shopped at this store," etc., until she was able to build enough ballast to support her spectacular English skin, fabulous facial bones and regal carriage.

There was another actor that I worked with who has done very well, who presented another kind of Hit problem. When I brought him up to York University to act in a play, my brilliant administrative assistant, Hazel Da Breo, labeled him as "the most beautifully cruel Greek man" she'd ever seen. Blond, blue eyes and incredibly thin lips. When he and I worked together I constantly had him move his State of Being to the right, since his Hit alone moved him very far to the left. If he didn't do that in a scene where he buys a hot dog from a street vendor, we'd worry for the life of the street vendor should any little thing be wrong with the wiener or one of the condiments.

Great actors also break the boundaries of Hits. Before Raul Julia, Puerto Ricans were usually portrayed as street thugs or hopeless drug addicts. When Harrison Ford got the rights to *Presumed Innocent* and could have hired any actor in the world to play opposite him — he chose Raul Julia.

When you arrive on set for the first time and go into hair and makeup to meet your acting partner, you're there to read their Hit and hear what they sound like. If there is supposed to be a familial relationship between you and the other actor, see if the Hits "hold." For example, if he's supposed to be your son, is there any family resemblance? If not, then you'll have to play him as your son in every scene, thus losing one of the major modifiers of Action — relationship.

As the world changes our vision of Hits will change. Had the American Iraq fiasco worked out the way they wanted, then men who looked like Donald Rumsfeld would be the image of wise elder statesmen — instead they look like old fools. America generates myths at a startling pace, and myths change our vision of Hits. Although it's not fun, actors need to periodically watch the TV news and see what the world is thinking because it can change the basics of how Hits work.

SOME EFFECTS OF CIVILITY ON ARTISTS

I moved back to Toronto when I had children because I wanted to raise them in the civility of Toronto. I remember my daughter, Beth, coming home from grade three one day to tattle on her brother — that he had a girlfriend. Naturally I wanted to know what she was like. Beth began by saying that she had a great back-pack. That she was a Black girl came fourth or fifth in her description — so Toronto is doing something right, civil-wise.

But civility and art don't always go hand in hand. Sometimes I feel that Toronto's civility comes about because we *ignore* difference. A seventy-year-old white man passes by a seventeen-year-old Korean woman and they both agree to just call each other people. Civil. But from an artist's perspective not really true. This is the agreement to *not* see — and if you don't see you can't be Present! The artist needs to acknowledge difference but see behind it to the person inside. To quote Naheed Nenshi, the mayor of Calgary, "I don't care what's *on* a person's head, I care what's *in* that head." But I would add: I don't ignore what's on the person's head either. I allow my class to see that I am a seventy-year-old Jew, but insist that they see behind whatever preconception they may have and see me as myself, but not independent of being a seventy-year-old Jew.

TO SUM UP:

1. Hits consist of country vs city, age up vs down, class up vs down, married vs single.
2. We are not necessarily our Hits, but we have to learn to play our Hits because it's the way into this industry.

3. Your Hit is the canvas upon which you are going to apply paint (modulations) and it ain't neutral.
4. Civility has its advantages and disadvantages.

CHAPTER 14

The Elephant in the Room

Probably time for me to address what for some (mostly older) actors, is the elephant in the room: What is the place of the theater in all this?

To be completely transparent — or as transparent as I am capable of being — I came from the theater. I have an MFA in Directing from the Yale School of Drama and have directed in major regional theaters and on Broadway. I also was the artistic director of a regional theater and directed the first Canadian play in the People's Republic of China. So, I do have some legitimate theater cred, but the world for professional actors has changed radically from what it was when I graduated in 1976.

The theater remains the mother art form and I always suggest that actors return to the theater periodically, but I think the financial realities of the present make it crucial that a professional actor finds a way to get cast in television and film.

Many of the actors I work with now think of the theater as an avocation not a vocation. They only take contracts in the theater if they really want the role, with people they respect and at times that fit their television and film shooting schedules. Often, they are willing to return their salaries to the regional theaters, all of which are struggling financially.

While television was just the basic broadcast channels, actors could claim that there was very little or no art to the writing on TV. But now, with streaming television and the new realities of making film, theater's claim to be *real* art compared to television and film simply no longer holds water.

Major writers now work in television and film. When premier novelists Dennis Lehane and Richard Price agree to write for series television and Noah Hawley (whose novel *Before the Fall* is sensational) show runs a series for HBO, then something serious has changed.

Major talents now realize that premium cable television has changed everything for the writing artist. They now have up to twenty-two hours to unwind their stories. The writing for *The Wire*, *The Sopranos*, the first season of *True Detective*, *Succession*, *Broadchurch*, *Breaking Bad*, *Fleabag*, *Queen's Gambit*, *The Crown*, *Bodyguard* and *Better Things* are just a few of the truly excellent shows available on the small screen. The stage is becoming more and more the place of events or evenings that resemble light opera, where skill is the prominent display.

The naturalism of Arthur Miller would now be better seen — and seen by many more people and more accurately — on television.

Because most streaming television production has to be careful of its costs, a lot of it consists of two actors talking across a table. (As an aside: every time an actor brings a script to me to prep that they are really excited about, it's always cheap — actors like those scripts because they get to talk — and talk is, as they say, cheap.) But these "talky" scripts also demand that the actors really know what they are doing to hold the attention of the audience. Take a look at the episode of *Chernobyl* where Jared Harris has about a forty-minute monologue that holds us transfixed (State of Being: I AM FALLING; Action: TO OPEN THE MINDS OF THOSE TO THEIR GUILT; relationship: older brother/younger brother).

Several prominent actors have gone so far as to say that they prefer working on film and TV over working on the stage, and it's almost always for the same reason: "The audience can really see what I'm doing" — allowing them to play micro-beats that the audience in a theater would never be able to see. Look at the extraordinary subtlety of the acting in *The Two Popes*.

If you look at the entirety of Stanislavski's work (and it is a remarkably large oeuvre) it can be distilled down to three crucial ideas. First, how to generate feeling in yourself — the generating of States of Being; second, the generating of feeling in your acting partner — the playing of Actions (you make your partner feel X so that they will do Y); and third, how to deliver the moment the two actors have created to the watching audience.

The camera allows you to ignore the third principle, as it "collects" moments between the actors without actors needing to figure out how to deliver them to the viewer.

I can't count the number of times, while directing in the theater, I'd have to hop onto the stage and congratulate the actors for finding something interesting and then had to add, "Now let's try to share it with the audience or let's cut it." A television or film director never has to have that nasty moment.

So, to sum up, if you want to work in the theater rather than on camera because the writing is better, then you'd better reevaluate. If you want to work in the theater because it is a more rewarding experience for you, then fine. If you want to make a living in the theater, I suggest you look at the reality of real estate not just in Toronto but in all of North America.

I think it's important for artists to be part of the world in which they live and not separated from it. Having the little amount of money that theater provides often puts an actor outside the life of the majority of people in the western world. Like it or not, those people are your audience. And even if you don't believe what they believe, their sheer numbers make you, at the very least, need to listen to their version of how the world works.

And hiding away in "festival" theaters where you are in a small town for eight or nine months of the year in some ways just delays the inevitable need to go to bigger cities and get involved in film or television — and the world as it really exists. Extended runs in New York or London are an exception. They pay reasonably well and can expose your talent to new groups of producers and showrunners from TV and film — and you get to live in the place where your art came from.

For years, when Perry Schneiderman (the finest theater administrator I've ever met) ran the National Theatre School of Canada, I was the last teacher those students saw before they graduated. After three years in a theater bubble they were "exposed" to me. I would mention that most real people don't wear leotards all the time, that getting a haircut is not a sin, that high-heeled shoes are a must for certain characters, that makeup was not fakery, that the gym was their best friend, that they had to treat their bodies like athletes treat theirs, etc. They would hate me for a full hour then realize that I was just trying to prepare them to make a living in their chosen profession.

In the first scene I'd have them do, I took the cameras off their dollies and taped over the zoom so that all they got to see was exactly what the audience saw. Many were shocked: "I don't act that badly" was a common refrain. And no, they didn't act that badly, but they acted on camera as they would on a stage in a large theater — Action first with State of Being (when they actually bothered with one) duplicating the information of the Action which promptly made them go over the top. (See the section on sequencing in chapter five.) It always took a few days to convince them to start with State of Being — and to find Primaries. Once they did, they acted well on camera and saw the joy of allowing the audience to actually see what they had found (into the valley, find and return to the fire). The students at the National Theatre School of Canada are an elite group of young actors who have, on the whole, done quite well in the profession.

Many have sought me out after they graduated to continue their training.

TO SUM UP:

1. Theater no longer has the cachet of all the great writers.
2. We can see an actor's work much better on camera than in the theater.
3. If you want to work in the theater rather than on camera because the writing is better, then you ought to reevaluate.
4. It's important for artists to be part of the world they live in and not separated from it.

CHAPTER 15

Principle #5 —
Icon and Action Not the Word

This is the hardest one for stage actors. Stage actors seek out the truth in what is being said by them and about them. Because I don't believe this is a valid approach, I start stage actors by working on Pinter's *Betrayal,* where virtually everyone lies about everything. So, the truth can only be found in the Action and the Icon, not the word.

For those of you old enough to remember, President Nixon drilled the final nails into the coffin of the "word as truth," and of course now we have the charming idea of "alternative facts." The truth is not contained always in the word, and TV and film actors know this. The truth is in the Action (that which you want from your acting partner) and the Icon (the name of the scene you are playing). In both cases it allows you to sidestep the specifics of text to find the truth beneath.

We dealt with Actions in chapter five — once again it is the metaphor of the Action, not the plot function of the Action that actors work on. We also touched on Icons, the names of scenes. Here's a fuller list of potential Icons:

- Firsts: First Date, First Kiss, First Time
- Is There a Future in This?
- The Marriage Proposal
- Meet the Family
- The Wedding
- I'm Pregnant
- The Morning After
- The Goodbye
- The Sacrifice (hurts me, helps you)
- The Crunch (hurt or be hurt)
- The Annunciation (and so it begins)
- The Revelation (finding a truth outside yourself)
- The Epiphany (finding a truth inside yourself)
- The Resurrection (a rekindling of life or love in yourself or in another for you)
- The Birthday
- The Anniversary
- Seeking Oblivion
- Seeking Safety (going home)
- The Homecoming
- The Holiday (a pause)
- The Temptation
- The Betrayal
- The Confrontation
- The Confession
- The Absolution
- The Appeal
- The Bet
- Gotcha

- The Bargain
- Friday at 4:45 p.m. (almost over)
- Monday at 7:15 a.m. (it's beginning again)
- In the Presence of Something Greater (god/ natural phenomena)

Both the Action and the Icon are indicators of what is really happening in a scene. The words — well, they are just words. (I'm allowed to say that because I make at least part of my living writing words and have a deep belief in them — but not for actors.)

The first time you're on set with a sensationally centered and Present actor you can't believe that right in the middle of the scene (where they have completely sucked you in) they turn and say, "What do I say next?" The words are not of prime importance to them. If they're sitting in the right State of Being and swinging on the Action, they're almost all the way home — the words can come later.

For example, take a scene where a man and woman go skating at an outdoor rink on a first date then sit at a table by the boards with cups of coffee in their hands. Actually, coffee in one hand — the other is sorta flopped on the table, inviting the other flopped hand to intertwine fingers. But the dialogue has nothing to do with fingers near each other on a table. The dialogue basically goes: "You're a really good skater." "Well, thanks, but you're a really good skater." "But not as good as you, who are a really good skater" — and on and on about skating. But the scene is not about skating. It's not about giving compliments. It's about the Icon — First Touch. Their hands are only inches apart, but they can't figure out how to cross those inches. No writer, no matter how good, can write you across those inches — those inches are actor territory.

As another example: The basic pickup works on a sequence of Icons — whether from a man to a woman or vice versa or any other gender configuration — and the Icons line up this way: 1) Can I Stand Near You? If the other person does not move away then the answer is yes. 2) Can I Talk to You? If the other person responds, then the answer is yes. 3) Can I Mention Something a Bit Suggestive? If they respond positively then the answer is yes. 4) A Seemingly Casual First Touch, and so on — by the way we are many, many yeses away from a bedroom. I also grant that Tinder changes the rules, but you still deal with First Touch, First Kiss, First Time, Morning After, etc.

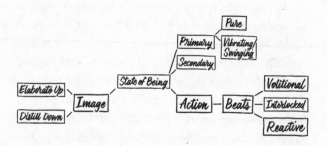

TO SUM UP:

1. The truth is in the Action and the Icon, *not* the word.

2. I'm going to repeat myself here and in item 3 and item 4 because I think it's important. Find the metaphor of the Action first and foremost. See what you know about the metaphor (opening someone's eyes for instance) in your own life independent of the script. Find the music, the poetry, the dance — the hockey stick — anything to enlarge your knowledge of the Action.

3. Everything springs from the Action. If it's on the left you want a State of Being on the right.

4. If the metaphor of the Action is in your head but not your heart you want the easy modifiers. If it's in your heart you use the hard modifiers (see previous chapter on Be Compelling, Not Right).

5. Then find the Icon and research it the same way you do the Action.

CHAPTER 16

Principle #6 —
Naturalism Not Realism

Professional actors need to be able to look like civilians (nonactors) and talk like civilians, but they have to have an artist's heart. The quintessential difference has to do with naturalism vs realism. In naturalism — which is almost exclusively what TV and film actors do — you must remain Present. In realism we are constantly avoiding being Present to prevent being hurt.

You must be recognizable to the viewing public and at the same time different from the audience who consumes your product — by the by, acting is the second most consumed of all the arts, pop music beats you guys hands down, sorry.

For example (to repeat myself) — in the great breakup scenes of your real life you drop into brother/sister (or any other sibling configuration you want) in order to protect yourself — realism. In TV and film we insist you stay in lover/lover (in fact you adore them more and more as they are breaking up with you) *and* be Present so that each of the "slings and arrows" pierces your heart.

It's at least part of what we pay you for. We haven't progressed that far from the gladiatorial arena when you think about it. The audience gets to cheer and be thrilled and be entirely safe; you get to be destroyed or rise to heaven for their edification.

As we've seen, this principle stops actors from accessing their behavior in order to find the truth. The truth — in Present tense — is deeper than your behavior and lives in a dark room protected by many dragons. It is quintessentially why your art form exists. It's what contributes to human growth and enhances the very nature of our lives. Prize it.

TO SUM UP:

1. Actors work in naturalism not realism.
2. Be Present for all the "slings and arrows."

CHAPTER 17

Auditions

Well, at last we come to something that has little to do with art but a ton to do with the business end of your world — auditions.

Although auditioning is not really acting (since it is all product and no process), you don't get to *really* act until you can figure out how to audition — do it well and actually enjoy it. After all, people fought to get you into that room or the right to self-tape, and casting directors are the guardians at the gates.

So, here are the principles:

1. **You must convert the audition room from a place of judgment to a business meeting.** The only question that must be in the air is whether what you are selling is what they are buying — not — whether what you are selling is any good. If you have any doubts about the quality of what you are selling, *DON'T GO INTO THE ROOM!*
2. **Almost no casting director can tell you how to act better, but they can evaluate what you put in front of them vis-à-vis what they are casting.** An

audition is *not* an evaluation of your acting talent! Don't make it one. That's a very fast track to hell.

3. **Every casting director has a different set of criteria.** In Los Angeles, on occasion I allow casting directors to come to class. They all want ten minutes to talk at the end. Ten minutes for a casting director is basically a half an hour. And each and every one of them lay out what they think an actor should do in the room: act directly to the casting director; never look at the casting director; I hate it when an actor asks questions; why don't actors ask questions?; don't use props; why don't actors use props? You get the gist. Your agent should be able to give you a hint or two as to what any particular casting director likes/wants. But their likes or wants have nothing to do with your talent.

4. **An audition is a business meeting.** They may make you feel like they are doing you a favor even bothering to see you, but the truth is that's their job — they get paid to see you and to determine if what you are selling is what their client is buying.

5. **You are selling your ethos not your ability to act.** The number of times that well-trained and talented actors get beaten for a role by eccentric backup singers from unknown rock bands is legion. They may be untrained, but they are willing to put their secrets out there for the world to see.

6. **There are two kinds of auditioning.** When a casting director knows you (i.e., has called you in a second time), then your audition is about whether you are right for the specific role. But if a casting director has *never* seen you before, all that you're trying to do is show them who you are, that you are interesting and someone they should get to know. So, in such auditions if there's something in the text (written in accent, very odd phrasing or some kinds of cursing) that throws you off your center, *don't do it*. When you first meet a casting director don't do *anything* that makes you look like a bad actor. Your Action is to get them to bring you back another time, to gain credit. To get back into the room, you must prove to them that you are a centered, compelling actor.

7. **To make an acting moment real it has to be to a specific person, for a specific reason and in a specific place.** In this the audition room poses two problems. The reader is most often banally neutral (better than them trying to outact you!) and the audition room is not a real place. The Action you can control, the partner you can't, but by use of a prop you can give us a sense of place. Two out of three should give you a leg up.

8. **Understand and utilize audition geography.** The standard opening shot is from your knees to just above your head. As the audition proceeds the

shot zooms in for women either just above or just below the chest — for men right across the chest. It's often best not to enter the frame. Just start in the frame turned three-quarters away from the camera, then turn toward the camera rather than making an entrance.

The geography is crucial. If you are standing the reader must stand. If you are seated the reader must sit. In both cases the reader has to be tight to the camera. Play to the reader not the camera unless instructed otherwise (more self-tape rules follow later in this chapter).

Here's how the geography works with the reader close to the camera. Real rooms are basically defined by the position of a door (either an exit or a way to a bedroom or deeper into the house) and the position of a window. So the geography is: door to reader to camera to window. (Diagram it if this is hard to follow.) The reader tosses you a line and you have an impulse to leave (i.e., turn toward the door) but decide to stay and you pan past the reader, past the camera and take your thought moment out the window. Swing, then decide to respond, then pan back past the camera, to the reader and say your line. That allows the camera to "find" you and to look at you in both profiles.

So those are the base principles — here are the rules, thoughts, ideas:

1. **Prepping:** For big auditions you need to be prepped because auditions are about product not process. Find someone who knows what they are doing so you go into the room with some sort of strategy and ready to present. Also be ready to cast aside all that you prepped if the auditioner has a different take on the scene than you prepared. This only applies to big auditions because prepping can be pricey — no point in paying for prepping small ones.

2. **Audition classes:** Audition classes are a total waste of money and time unless it is a casting director you've always wanted to meet and this is the only way to meet them. Audition classes are illegal in California — they are classified as pay for play and should be classified as such in Canada. In Toronto, it's a waste of time to take a class from an American casting director because they can't cast you! American casting directors, now that they can't do classes in California, have found Canada a rich source of gullible young actors. Beware!

3. **Know the show:** Find a way to watch at least a part of an episode of the show you are auditioning for, to get the tone if nothing else. It's also respectful. For film auditions, know the director's credits.

4. **Dress the class structure of the character:** No more jeans and sports coats for men. We'll forgive you for not having cordovan shoes

when you audition for lawyers, but no runners! Strangely, and I can't explain this, casting directors get offended when you wear scrubs when auditioning for doctors and nurses. Haven't really figured that one out.

5. **Casting directors are not paid to be imaginative:** It's your business to know if you should be wearing a hat, if you should have your hair up, etc.

6. **Self-taping:** There are some actors who prefer to self-tape rather than go into the room, and there are some shows that cast only from self-tapes. If you are going to self-tape don't go to the factory self-tape places. You're only money to them, and they rush you through. They claim to supply readers for you, but their readers aren't actors. A waste of money. There are many private studios that do self-tapes and take it seriously. Often, in Toronto, very talented actors like Noam Jenkins and Nola Auguston offer self-tape services where they not only shoot you, they also coach you and read for you. They're not on the clock like the factory places — going over time isn't usually a big deal to them.

You can also self-tape at home with a cell phone. Just be careful to get enough light when you do and follow any directions about the self-taping that come with the taping request.

Almost without exception when you self-tape the first or the third take will be the best you can do. The first because it's fresh, the second is usually awful as you try to regain what you found in the first, and the third is better because you go "fuck it, let's shoot!"

When self-taping you have to direct the reader to toss their lines exactly as you want them. An audition is like slow-pitch baseball — they lob the line across the plate and you smack it out of the park. For self-tapes you have to dress and prop the scene, especially if you do it at home. Be sure there is enough light!

If you're sending self-tapes to Los Angeles be aware that they can receive a thousand tapes per role. The tapes aren't usually watched by the casting director but by their assistant, who views them on fast-forward just attempting to cut it down to twenty or thirty tapes for the casting director to look at. That being the case, put everything important into the first four lines, 'cause they ain't going to watch more than that at first.

Lastly, don't eye lock the camera when you self-tape.

7. **Callbacks:** There are rarely callbacks in Toronto, so no scripts the first time into the room. In most other places there are callbacks, but even then on your first audition you can hold the script but never look at it. Holding the script does two good things. It lowers expectation and tells you what to do with your right hand (if you're right-handed). Some teachers preach

that you should hold the script then look down, get your line, then look up and speak. I've never seen an actor able to do this and still be Present.

8. **Waiting room:** Older actors are completely aware that if you get the role they do not and they sometimes try to psych you out. So, get a large set of headphones and tuck the cord — if there is a cord — in your shirt. Or go to the person at the desk and ask how the timing is going. If you're not up for half an hour, take a walk.

9. **Slate (if they'll let you):** It's an opportunity to casually say hello. Don't proclaim, just say hi and tell them your name and agency and any other info they want. You always have to slate on self-tapes. It's a genial way to start an audition. If you have a complicated or uncommon name, then say your name slowly, otherwise your entire audition could be them trying to figure out what your name is instead of listening and watching you.

10. **Glad-handing:** I think it a bad idea for Canadian actors to glad-hand as they enter the room. A quiet, secure smile that you are happy to see them is enough.

11. **Props:** I say use them. They have to fit in your pocket or you can carry them in one hand. They are there to help you establish place. It's why God made neckties for men and long hair for women. It's surprising how good a cop scene becomes when the actor is sitting at a table eating from a take-out Chinese food container.

12. **Use of guns:** Nothing that can be a real weapon should enter a casting room, but fingers pointing are not a gun. *There's no miming in an audition room.* Bring in something that is clearly not a weapon and show them that this is what you are going to use as a gun.

13. **Use of cigarettes:** It will be made clear in the audition notice if you have to smoke in the role. If you won't, don't go in the room. They do not want you to light up in the audition room but, yes, you should pull out a cigarette and pop it in your mouth and cup your hands as if you're lighting it. (I know I just said no miming — this is the exception.)

14. **Can I ask questions?** Yep, two — and they have to have yes or no answers.

15. **Can I start over?** Well if it's really awful, sure, why not. Can I restart a second time? Nope, you're done. Better to leave no impression than a bad one.

16. **Can I take a moment?** No! They made you wait for forty fucking minutes, how many moments do you want?

17. **Kissing scenes:** Yep, they ask you to do scenes that include kissing. Do you pucker? I guess. But the acting moments are before and after the kiss: the decision to kiss, then what you learned on the kiss.

18. **Violent scenes:** Yep, they ask you to pull out your liver and shove it in your ear. All I can say

about stuff like that is — throw yourself at it but don't hurt yourself.

19. **Big emotional scenes:** Yep, they'll ask you to do the hard scenes. They have to be sure that you can get to the required emotion in the casting room because on set there may be no one able to help you with it.

20. **Nudity:** Well I wish there was a thing called "tasteful nudity," but the words "tasteful" and "nudity" go together like the words "Brooklyn" and "Yankees" — they don't. If you are not willing to remove your clothes I think that's fine assuming: a) that you and your agent have an understanding about this and that you don't go into rooms where the role clearly indicates that you have to remove your clothes and b) you know why.

   If your answer to b) is that real actors don't remove their clothes, then I think you have to reconsider this because so many very talented actors for the sake of the project have removed their clothing. Bad actors who take off their clothes are simply naked bad actors. Good actors who remove their clothing remain good actors. Unless you are really hard up for rent there is no reason to take roles where there's nothing there but your nudity. But being hard up for rent can be real.

   However, if the role is good and there's a nude scene, *do* have a good reason not to proceed.

On the whole, scripts and casting directors make it perfectly clear what is required and you have to sign off on the nudity clause. And yeah, you get a few extra shekels. But when it comes to doing the shot, you mustn't balk or there will be hell to pay — they played fair with you about it. You are always welcome to have union reps on the set to make sure that you're safe and the set will be brought down to its lowest possible numbers — and after it's done, they'll applaud you.

Beware: nonunion shooting or shooting in districts with less powerful unions leave a performer little protection if there is the call for nudity. So take care.

21. **Religious beliefs:** I have several evangelical actors at my studio in Toronto. They won't say bad words, won't do scenes that oppose their religious views, often won't act with members of the opposite sex to whom they are not married. Again, just be honest with your agent and don't appear in casting rooms where, if you got the role, you'd refuse it on religious grounds.

22. **Dyslexia:** A lot of talented actors are dyslexic. You and your agent have to be upfront about this. Most casting directors will offer you more time to prepare.

23. **When the reader makes a mistake:** About 15 percent of the time the reader, especially after a long day, makes a mistake and either skips lines or more likely reads your line. Don't lose your

cookies! Smile, and practice saying, "That's a very good read, but I believe that's my line. Can we start again?"

24. **Be compelling, not necessarily right** — *but not eccentric.* This is covered more extensively in chapter eight.

25. **Angry audition rooms:** Some audition rooms have gotten kinda angry. Ignore it as much as you can. Casting directors are sometimes monetarily squeezed by producers — they aren't really angry with you.

26. **Prove that you're happy to see them:** They know you don't like waiting or being judged, but if you can't prove to them that you are happy to see them then they think you can't act.

27. **Play to the person in the room who likes you:** If there are three people behind the desk, one got you into the room and thinks you're special, one thinks you're less than nothing special and one doesn't know you. Don't try to convince the one who doesn't like you that they ought to. They've gone on record as saying you are a jerk or the like, so ignore them.

28. **It is not possible to be loved by all casting directors** but you need a coterie of them who call you in over and over again if you want to make a living at this.

29. **The casting line:** There is a line in the script that if you can't say believably then you can't get cast. Even if you have the agent from hell who calls

you at 7:30 for an 8:30 audition, you still have time to find the casting line and do some work on it so that it applies correctly to you. It's an audition tool.

30. **Play a volitional first beat no matter how it's written:** If the opening line from the reader is "How are you?" and your response is "Fine." In real acting you would be in interlock with your partner (see chapter five), but this is an audition, so you want the first thing out of your mouth to be in volition. Think of it like tennis: if you return the serve simply trying to keep the ball in the court — you are in interlock — but in volition you allow the serve to land, ignore it and hear it rattling against the chain-link fence behind you, then reach into your pocket and pull out a ball and serve — in volition. Being in volition, no matter what the text has you say first, announces, *my audition, watch me.*

31. **The State of Being of all auditioning is I AM WORTHY:** Even if the character is written as a weakling, you're going to show them that your version of weakling is very worthy of their attention. Actors need to remember that even cheap shooting can cost five or six hundred dollars an hour — so be worth it!

32. **Your acting partner is actually the power in the room** *not* **the reader:** Your Action: if you had the right to determine the end of the scene your

acting partner would jump on the table and exclaim, "Where the fuck have you been all my life! I have a new series shooting in Paris and you'd be perfect for the lead!"

33. **Make the character modulations** — age up/down, country/city, class up/down, married/single — outside the audition room so that you enter in character.

34. **Get your hands up into the frame early in the take:** Once the camera has zoomed into the close-up you are like a talking head on a newscast. Putting your hand/s up in the frame reaffirms your full self — note Brando's endless touching of his face.

35. **If there's a preconception about you and your work then you have to play against it:** If you have a lot of modeling in your résumé, you have to prove to them that you have emotional depth. The rap against models is that they don't feel anything. If your résumé is heavy with classical theater work then you have to prove that you can act without rhythm or rhyme. If you have a lot of dance on your résumé you have to prove to them that you can handle text and that you don't need someone shouting "Five, six, seven, eight" before you can perform.

36. **Agent feedback:** So this one always gets me into trouble. But if you've been going into the room over and over again and feeling that you are doing really well but getting nothing

in return (callbacks, pinned, casted) then I guarantee you that something is happening in the room that you don't understand, and it becomes the best reason to have a powerful agent (one who has clients who are stars). They can get on the phone and demand to know what's happening in your audition. Now, the casting director doesn't like this conversation but the sotto voce is that if the casting director doesn't answer your agent's question then the next time the casting director wants a star on your agent's roster, they are just not going to be available. So, the casting director gingerly answers the question, "They've gotten a little bitter don't you think?" A little bitter — the kiss of death. Your personal life has gone to rat shit and when you breathe down it feels Present, but you are inadvertently channeling bile. Your auditions feel good — but they are not good, they are bitter. Then of course there's "What's with his haircut, what's with her makeup, he needs to go to the gym, is she still smoking, etc." All things you wouldn't consider and only a powerful agent can find out for you.

37. **Find a silence early in the take and swing in a Primary State of Being:** Remember that if you want to play leads you have to interest us in what you think, not just what you do.

38. **Drone Note in from the top:** See chapter nine for more detail.

39. **Don't use the chair unless it's a scene that demands that you sit:** Here's something simple and practical —the best thing to do with a chair is to stand behind it with your hands on the chair back.

40. **Allow the camera to see you:** Sounds simple, but it takes a twist in your thinking to allow in a neutral observer.

41. **Eye line:** There actually is a guy who taught an "eye line" class. Here it is: if you stand the reader must stand, if you sit the reader must sit-pas de plus. Young actors beware.

42. **Multiple reader roles:** If the reader reads more than one role and all the roles are equal, then place them all on one side of the camera — stack 'em up. But if only a line or two come from another character put that character across the camera.

43. **Auditions for firsts vs seconds vs thirds:** With firsts they want to see you think, with seconds they want to see you do and with thirds they want character totally based on behavior. This is covered in chapter ten.

44. **Claim the ground:** The room should be different when you leave it, not like a British butler whose claim to fame is that he comes and he goes and the room always remains the same.

45. **Keep your opinions to yourself:** If you have a powerful enough agent to get you the full script, read it! But be careful of directors or

showrunners who ask what you think of the script. It's awful to say, but play dumb. "It's interesting, I can really see great things," etc. If you really get involved in a conversation about the script you will probably get yourself uncast because they don't really care what the fuck you think of the script.

46. **Keep your technique to yourself:** Be careful. If they ask you how you like to work, once again say something dumb like, "I like a lot of attention" or "I read the words and react to them." There are many directors who don't like the idea that actors actually know what they are doing.

47. **Clarify pronunciation:** Find a site on the internet that gives you proper American and/or British pronunciation of all words. Use it — especially for doctor and sci-fi shows.

48. **Reading with the casting director:** When the casting director reads with you rather than a reader, you have to quickly determine whether the casting director is sending clean signal or not (i.e., are they being truthful). If they are sending clean signal, then away you go. If they are not, if they are schmackting, then you have to make up what their line readings mean and — well, you're literally on your own.

49. **Pair auditions:** Some Los Angeles audition rooms like to audition pairs of actors at the same time. Be aware that there is only one camera. If your acting partner heads upstage

(look it up) then you have to follow upstage or else your entire shot is the back of your head.

50. **"That's a really good scene"**: If you hear those words as you leave the room, you've lost. You want them talking about you — you are not to subordinate yourself to the text.

51. **Second callbacks (your third time in the room)**: When there is a second callback, it is the first time they really want you to act. You walk into the room and there's a guy with a slender body and big head — he's the lead and he's cast. Now they want to see if you can find (have chemistry with) him. If he's an American, you can be pretty sure that he'll go off text and want you to improvise with him. If he's a Brit, word perfect, please. But for the first time in the audition room you are being asked to find product off of another actor — process not product is what's wanted. In Canada if he is an American, he may have casting privilege — in other words, he gets to say yes or no to you.

52. **Final auditions for big films are often just you and the director**: No camera, no casting director. They just want to talk. They have already made up their mind that you're capable of doing the role. Now they want to know something about you, so do have something to say but stay away from politics and religion. Republicans often only hire Republicans just as Democrats often only hire Democrats. And you

would be surprised how many of your favorite actors are Republicans!

53. **Reward yourself if you do well in the audition room:** If you were able to get Present and show them who you really are, reward yourself — not with food!

A WORD OR TWO ABOUT PHOTOGRAPHS

Yes, you need to get photos done by a professional photographer. And, no, it's not good enough to just have them on your computer. And yes, you need to bring your photos to the audition room.

There are two different kinds of photos for actors to consider. If you're just starting out and you're using the photo to try and get an agent, don't spend a lot of money on the picture because most good agents are going to want you to reshoot to their specifications anyway.

It's best to get photos that are not copy protected by the photographer — after all you paid for it, it's yours. Copy-protected copies are more expensive as well.

No one gets a job because of a great photo, but lots of folks don't even get into the audition room because their photo isn't good enough.

DON'T GLAM! The photo should look like you. Having a photo that advertises you as something that you are not can seriously annoy casting directors.

Don't get character photos (you dressed as a cop or a mobster or a doctor). Your photo should be just you relaxed and Present *and* dressed in the appropriate class structure for your casting.

It's very hard for young actors to get a good photo. The whole situation can be quite intimidating, but you need to make the photographer "dance with you" not "dance on you."

CHAPTER 18

When the Moon's Too Thin for Stories

When the Moon's Too Thin for Stories was the subtitle of one of my novels. The editor wanted to know exactly what it meant. I couldn't explain it then, nor can I now — *but* it touches me and allows me to put thinking and feeling together.

I believe it's important for artists to keep such catch-phrases/touchstones — those that move them even if they don't know why — and just sit with them, and grow from them. I grant that I come from a time when the written word meant more than it does today, but I would argue that we've never found anything that replaces what the written word does for artists.

Here are a few more: "For fear of nightmares, humanity will abandon dreaming, just watch them." I believe I read that on a subway wall in Brooklyn sometime in the late '70s and it stuck with me. In fact, it was the inspiration for my sci-fi series The Dream Chronicles.

Then there's this one: "Good stories reveal truths, but are not necessarily truthful" — I used a variant of that at the very beginning of this book.

And this: "Fiction is only truth filtered through a creative mind."

And now some more advice to actors:

1. Think the thought, swallow the thought, then just say the stupid words. If you act *on* the word or play *with* the words to make them mean more, then you are doing Victorian stage acting.
2. Thoughts travel, not words.
3. Embrace the contradiction of swinging (or the depth of the Drone Note), allow it to boil inside you. Just before it gets to be too much (i.e., you wouldn't be able to say your lines), put the lid on. If you put the lid on too soon you've stopped your growth.
4. You have to look like civilians, talk like civilians but have an artist's heart — again something I've mentioned before.

Here are two more that are hung on my studio door — the first is by the famous acting teacher Uta Hagen commenting on her book.

I called the book *Respect for Acting*. I did not call the book delight in acting or the fun of acting. I don't care about that. I care about work and responsibility and the truth and commitment.

The second is:

I can't fathom why actors allow their profession to be called a craft. An actor playing Benvolio has a hell of lot more to do with the success or failure of his production of *Romeo and Juliet* than the third violinist in the orchestra does in his production of the ballet of *Romeo and Juliet*. But a violinist would never ever say that what he or she does is a craft. It is an art. Period. So is acting.

That one's by me.

APPENDIX

Exercises

These exercises are for beginners and for teachers who want to teach this method. They coordinate with specific chapters as noted below.

CHAPTER 1: PRESENT TENSE

Take a walk down a crowded street. Allow yourself to see the tallest and shortest person. The fairest, the foulest. The thinnest, the thickest. Make yourself see the most desirable store, the worst place to live, the exact position of the sun. Stand still periodically and listen to the sound of your city. Stop for a moment and do a 360-degree turn and realize that you have just seen a vast panoply of humanity into which you must fit (look like them, sound like them but have an artist's heart) — and for whom you are going to venture into the dangerous valley and bring back something of value for them to see/hear/experience.

CHAPTER 3: DIRECT YOURSELF

Exercise #1: In the scene below, open the concrete nouns.
Exercise #2: In the scene below name the Action of both characters (the metaphoric Action).
Exercise #3: Name the States of Being.

```
INT. LOFT APARTMENT. AROUND 8:00 P.M.

B sits alone over a returned
manuscript and a rejection letter from
a publisher. A has already read the
rejection letter — it's unequivocal
and includes the phrase "please don't
send us any more of your work."

A comes out of the kitchen as B
throws the rejection letter into the
garbage with more than a little fury.
After a beat:

                A
     Maybe it just wasn't meant to
     be.

                B
     What does that mean?

                A
     Just what it says. Maybe. It.
     Just. Wasn't. Meant to be.

                B
     Christ, Jesus!

Long beat — A makes a decision.
```

                         A
          Look — I can't go through
          another month of you . . .
          [moping around]. We're not kids
          anymore. This isn't working
          for you. It's not making you
          happy. It's not. Be honest.
          This profession doesn't seem to
          want . . .

                         B
          What I write. Fucking
          publishers . . .

                         A
          Yeah, but who else sells books?

                         B
          They're idiots.

Beat, brave

                         A
          All of them are idiots? All of
          them?

                         B
          All of them.

                         A
          If they're idiots why do you
          care what they think? If you
          believe in your writing put it
          up on the web. Do a blog. Give
          it away for free. There are
          lots of ways of getting your
          stuff to the reading public.

                    B
          Did you read the last . . .

A nods.

                    B
          And did you like it?

Longest beat.

                    A
          No. I didn't like it, and yes,
          I understand why the publishers
          won't publish it.

                    B
          I see.

                    A
          Do you?

                    B
          Trust me I see.

A puts on a coat.

                    B
          Where're you going?

                    A
          Out. I need a . . . [break from
          all this]

                    B
          Where are . . .

                    A
          O'Malley's. They have a good

```
                    burger, a strong lager and
                    music. You used to love music.

                              B
                    Yeah. Do you . . . [want
                    company]

                              A
                    I have a right to a little
                    happiness too.

            A leaves.
```

CHAPTER 7: KEYING

Look seriously at the room in which you are sitting. Find the telling detail — the Key — that differentiates this room from other rooms. Open the Key. Now go into another room and activate the Key — see what it does to the second room.

CHAPTER 9: DRONE NOTING

Pick out the Drone Notes in the following scene for both actors. Hint: there is more than one Drone Note for each role. You start with one and once you get to that one you jump forward, emotionally, to the next Drone Note.

```
      INT. MIDDLE CLASS LIVING ROOM. 10:30
      P.M.

      The lead story of the evening news
      has just finished. The television is
```

on loud in the background. A scene
of appalling bloodshed is being put
into story form by a news network.
The scene picks up mid-argument —
actually there are only two lines
missing. A has said, "Now that's
bullshit." And B has replied, "Not
it's not, it's a matter of faith."

A
It's a matter of what?

B
Faith. You heard me the first
time.

A
It's a matter of faith?

B
Yes.

A
Faith — you mean believing?

B
You know I mean that.

A
Faith!

B
You say that like it's a curse.

A
Faith is all that is necessary
to be right. To be saved. To —

                    B
        To some, yes, faith is all you
        need.

                    A
        Good works mean nothing? Being
        a good person means nothing?

                    B
        Of course they do.

                    A
        But not as much as believing
        in the rituals? Doing the
        bullshit?

                    B
        Rituals are not bullshit.

Pause.

                    B (cont.)
        Forty-eight percent of North
        Americans identify themselves
        as born-again Christians. They
        have faith. They believe.

                    A
        In what? That gay people are
        evil, that sexuality needs to
        be covered and kept in the
        dark, that feminists are
        the devil's work, that women
        have no right to abortion and
        probably that the races should
        be separated.

After a pause.

                    B
        Many do believe those things.

                    A
        Because they are written in a
        book that may or may not even
        be remotely true.

                    B
        The book is true.

                    A
        The book is a fairy tale.

                    B
        You blaspheme.

                    A
        You refuse to discuss.

                    B
        There is no need to discuss
        faith. It exists. It is. It is
        an important part of my life —
        I never hid that from you.

A beat.

                    A
            (referring to the damage
            on the TV)
        Are there sacred places in the
        world?

                    B
        You know there are.

                    A
          Is the planet sacred?

                    B
          Beyond a doubt.

                    A
          But there are parts of the
          planet that are more sacred
          than other parts?

After a beat, knowing full well where
this is going:

                    B
          Yes.

                    A
          Some pieces of stupid rock on
          the earth are more sacred than
          other pieces of stupid rock on
          the earth?

                    B (carefully)
          Yes.

                    A
          So if we could have peace, if
          children could grow up without
          the fear of violence in their
          lives would you give up a piece
          of this sacred rock?

                    B
          In exchange for what? What do I
          get for my sacred piece of rock
          for violating the dictates of
          my faith?

                           A
         Peace.

                           B
         Peace to do what? Shop on the
         Sabbath? Choose between thirty-
         five flavors of ice cream? See
         three-quarters naked women
         on every cover, every billboard,
         every bus shelter. What, to get
         a new refrigerator every three
         years, a new car every five, a
         new house every ten. What is
         this peace for? My life is not
         about acquiring things. I am
         just fine with less. I'm not fine
         without my faith. And my faith
         needs ritual. And ritual needs
         those sacred places.

After a very long pause.

                           A
         I don't want any kid of ours
         inculcated with this crap.

                           B
         Religion is not crap.

                           A
         Organized religion is crap.

                           B
         Organized religion gives
         meaning to our days.

                           A
         "Crack open any stone and I am

```
                    there. Cut any piece of wood
                    and you will find me."

                                B
                    You can't quote when it suits
                    you and leave out the rest.

            Beat.

                                A
                    You can't force a child of ours
                    to follow your faith.

                                B
                    Just watch me.

            B exits. A is left with their thoughts.
```

CHAPTER 10: CHARACTER

Pick your favorite TV show or film. Watch the lead and define their choices, name the swing and go through the character modifiers to see how the actor has delineated their character. Then name the second and the third in the show.

CHAPTER 11: SELECTING NOT PRETENDING

Exercise #1: Sit on the subway and watch the passengers enter and exit. Find one or two who interest you and write their backstory: how did they get to sit on the subway that day; married/single, class structure, education level; what has happened to their life that thrilled them; what else happened that killed their dreams.

Exercise #2: While sitting on a bus or subway or restaurant spot an elderly man — it works best with an elderly man wearing religious garb. Imagine what they were like as a teenager, chasing girls, playing ball, being bad.

Exercise #3: Once you think you have the character under control, that you understand them, take them shopping. Shoe shopping is particularly good. Go to shops you never want to go back to because I'm going to ask you to try on every pair of shoes — in character — and buy none of them.

Exercise #4: This one is works best for most women. Kick out your roommates and have a serious glass or two of wine then go to your closet and from left to right pull out each piece of clothing and remember where you got it and who you were trying to impress at the time. Then do the same for your shoes, then your underclothing (often the most revelatory). Each piece of clothing links to a part of yourself and can be used when you select rather than pretend.

The reason it doesn't work for most (not all) men is that when they open their closets, they have jeans and T-shirts — not much to pick from there. Although if you are a male who has a ton of clothes then do the exercise the same as the women.

CHAPTER 12: TANGENT — VOICE IN YOUR HEAD

Read this script — hear the voice in your head — try to sidestep the voice as you self-tape both roles. Then

watch your self-tape and see if you've avoided the voice
in your head but still managed to get across the plot.

```
INT. A LAID-BACK COFFEE SHOP.
LATE AFTERNOON.

A is packing up after a very pleasant
half hour chat with B, who A has just
met. B is about to put a copy of the
New Yorker into their bag when:

                A
     That's my New Yorker.

                B
          (Extracting it from their
          bag)
     Sorry.

A looks at B for a long moment.

                A
     Were you going to take my New
     Yorker home?

                B
     It's rare you find a New Yorker
     in a coffee shop like this —
     copies of Metro, Now and other
     free junk, sure, but never a
     New Yorker.

                A
     So you were just going to take
     it?
```

                    B

    Yes, I was going to take it,
    read it then bring it back. I'm
    here almost every other day.

Pause.

                    A

    Really? You were going to bring
    it back?

                    B

    I said as much.

Pause.

                    A

    But it's my *New Yorker*.

                    B

    But I didn't know that. If I'd
    known that I'd never have taken
    it without asking.

Pause.

                    A

    I've enjoyed talking with you.
    You're smart.

                    B

    I hear a "but" at the end of
    your last sentence.

                    A

    There is.

                B

    "But" I took your *New Yorker*?

                A

    Yes.

                B

    But I didn't know it was yours.

                A

    And you were going to bring it
    back after you read it?

                B

    Right.

Long pause.

                B

    So you going to give me your
    phone number?

IF NO: A packs up, turns and goes,
forgetting the *New Yorker* on the
table. B picks up the *New Yorker* and
reads their name and address aloud
from the subscription sticker on the
magazine.

IF YES: A hands over a business card,
picks up the *New Yorker* and says:
"But it's still my *New Yorker*." And B
replies, "Now and always."

CHAPTER 10: NO NEUTRAL MASK

Back to the bus. Read the Hit of the bus driver, then the most elegantly dressed person on the bus, then the most modestly dressed person.

CHAPTER 11: ELEPHANT IN THE ROOM

Go to the theater and prove me wrong — but musicals don't count.

CHAPTER 15: THE ICON AND THE ACTION NOT THE WORD

Name the Actions and Icons for both characters in the following scene. Open the metaphor of the Action and do the same for the Icon.

```
INT. A SITTING ROOM. NIGHT

                A
    She was important to me.

Beat, B looks aghast at A

                A (cont.)
    She was. She's in my dreams.
    Every night I dream her. I
    close my eyes and she's there.
    Always there.

                B
    She's gone, pushing up the
```

daisies, singing off-key in the
devil's own quintet.

                    A
Don't do that. I cared about her.

                    B
You cared more about your
latest pair of shoes than you
ever cared about her. Why do
you lie about shit like this?
She was nothing to you. She's
dead now, but she's not worth
mourning. She wasn't even worth
enough for you to give her
the odd call. Fuck, I never
remember you even returning one
of her calls. Not even one. But
now that she's dead all of a
sudden you cared. You cared.

                    A
I care.

                    B
Changing the tense doesn't make
it more real. She was a bitch
on wheels. She hated you.

                    A
Maybe . . . but she despised
you.

                    B
Ah, now there's a truth.

Beat, then:

                        A
            Did you ever like her?

Beat then:

                        B
            Nope, not even for a second did
            I like her.

                        A
            She was my mother.

                        B
            Proving that any woman who can
            spread their legs can become a
            mom.

Beat, then:

                     B (cont.)
            Come on, [A's name], she was a
            jerk.

Beat, then:

                        A
            Yeah, my mother the jerk died.

CHAPTER 16: NATURALISM VS REALISM

Go back over your last breakup scene in real life.
Remember the moments that you were Present and
those that you were not.

CHAPTER 17: AUDITIONS

Go to WhySanity.net, pick out an audition piece and put it on tape. If the site asks you to send them your email address, don't, pick another piece.

AN AFTERWORD

I turned seventy this past January, and as Mark Twain said, "Once a person gets to be seventy they have the right to stand up on that ledge and tell us all how they got there. They all do it these garrulous old people. They explain the process and dwell on the particulars with senile rapture. I assume I achieved my seventy years in much the same way as everyone else by doing things that would have killed most everyone else. Come to think of it I did have to stop frolicking with mince pie after midnight last year — before then I didn't know it was loaded!"

Well, I think I achieved my seventy years with the help of the gracious, talented artists that I taught and directed, who always challenged me and kept me young enough to write this book.

DAVID ROTENBERG has been a master acting teacher for more than 30 years. He has directed on Broadway, in major regional theaters, for television and has an MFA in directing from the Yale School of Drama. David has taught at York University, the National Theatre School of Canada, the Shanghai Theatre Academy, the University of Cape Town and Princeton. He regularly teaches professional classes in Toronto, Vancouver and Los Angeles, plus Zoom classes with actors from four continents. His students included Tatiana Maslany, Rachel McAdams, Scott Speedman, Sarah Gadon, Ennis Esmer, Patrick Adams, David Hirsh, Jonas Chernick and Shawn Doyle. He is also the author of 11 novels, including the Dream Chronicles, the Junction Chronicles, the Zhong Fong Mysteries and the novel *Shanghai*. He directed the first Canadian play in the People's Republic of China — in Mandarin. He lives in Toronto, Canada, where he is the artistic director of the internationally known studio The Professional Actors Lab.

Purchase the print edition and receive the eBook free!
Just send an email to ebook@ecwpress.com and include:

- the book title
- the name of the store where you purchased it
- your receipt number
- your preference of file type: PDF or ePub

A real person will respond to your email with your eBook attached.
And thanks for supporting an independently owned Canadian publisher
with your purchase!